As I read *Big-Hearted People*, I couldn't help but imagine Randy as the loyal, loving, humble, and faithful scribe carefully attending to and reflecting back to what Jesus desires we all would know (and practice) about love. It's God's challenge that we find the courage to purposefully and authentically live the Big-Hearted life in difficult, big-headed times. This book will stir your soul to reflect on Jesus' teachings and, as a result, inspire you to open your heart to greater community and fellowship with others. Read this book and I bet you'll reexamine your life journey as a Big-Hearted Person of faith, hope, and love—knowing full well that the greatest of these is love.

—BOB DUBOIS, M.A., L.P.C.
PROFESSOR OF PSYCHOLOGY
WAUKESHA COUNTY TECHNICAL COLLEGE
MILWAUKEE, WISCONSIN

In this book *Big-Hearted People*, I see my life in many avenues. It draws a portrait of our lives, using scriptures, and characters of the Bible to illustrate what we should be like in this time upon earth. We defeat Satan as we become the Big-Hearted Person God intends for us to be. Personally knowing the author means so much as to the defining of its validity to the book. It captures the heart of the Father.

—PASTOR JIM WATSON
CROSSROADS FAMILY FELLOWSHIP
MONTVERDE, FLORIDA

Big-Hearted People goes to the center of what it means to be a Christian. The framework for this book is the author's own vivid experience of discovering the reality that "Big-Hearted People" make a difference in this world. He digs deep into the scriptures and brings up a treasure store of instruction and encouragement to share with the body of Christ. Its truths move me to God, and you will be moved too.

—DR. JAN L GARBER
PRESIDENT
VISION CHRISTIAN BIBLE COLLEGE AND SEMINARY
CLERMONT, FLORIDA

In the midst of cultural pressures which seek to promote self and preserve personal gain, it's imperative that we invest in content that reminds us to give our lives away for the sake of others. I can think of few more qualified books fit to such a task than Big-Hearted People. Randy is not only a masterful storyteller, but he is also a man who truly practices what he preaches. This is a work of experience, adorned with profound truth. Positive, uplifting, life-changing!

—CHRISTOPHER HOPPER

AUTHOR OF THE WHITE LION CHRONICLES AND

THE BERINFELL PROPHECIES

CLAYTON, NEW YORK

This book is a real blessing from God. It shows clearly from God's Word that when we truly repent, believe, and receive Christ, knowing who He really is and His finished work upon the cross, we become people who are Christ-Hearted (Big-Hearted). In this way God can use us to draw others into the kingdom of God. We are designed by God to demonstrate His love on this earth as it becomes a reality in our lives by allowing Christ to live in and through us.

—PASTOR RON LENAHAN

FAITH TO FAITH FELLOWSHIP

ROCHESTER, NEW YORK

Randy Schum goes right to the heart of the Christian matter, with a fresh, inspiring voice. I loved the peaceful harmony and rhythm of his message. When Randy encourages us to be Big-Hearted in our own unique ways, he is modeling for us his own desire not to be a stagnant reservoir, but a river of life for God's people. He is very direct, yet very gentle in guiding people. Kindness of spirit overflows throughout this book, and I am grateful for it.

—DIANE SCHNEIDER, J.D., PH.D.

THEOLOGIAN/HARP VIBRATION THERAPIST

ST. AUGUSTINE, FLORIDA

BIG-HEARTED
PEOPLE

Best Wishes,
Randy J. Schum

RANDY J. SCHUM

CREATION
HOUSE
A STRANG COMPANY

BIG-HEARTED PEOPLE by Randy J. Schum
Published by Creation House
A Strang Company
600 Rinehart Road
Lake Mary, Florida 32746
www.strangbookgroup.com

Scripture quotations marked THE MESSAGE are taken from *The Message: New Testament With Psalms and Proverbs* by Eugene H. Peterson. Copyright © 1993, 1994, 1995 by Eugene H. Peterson, NavPress, P.O. Box 35001, Colorado Springs, Colorado 80935.

Scripture quotations marked NIV are from the Holy Bible, New International Version of the Bible. Copyright © 1973, 1978, 1984, International Bible Society. Used by permission.

Scripture quotations marked NKJV are from the New King James Version of the Bible. Copyright © 1979, 1980, 1982 by Thomas Nelson, Inc., publishers. Used by permission.

Scripture quotations marked AMP are taken from the Amplified˚ Bible, Copyright © 1954, 1958, 1962, 1964, 1965, 1987 by The Lockman Foundation. Used with permission." (www.Lockman.org)

Scripture quotations marked KJV are from the King James Version of the Bible.

Scripture quotations marked NEW LIFE are taken from The Holy Bible, *NEW LIFE Version*. ©. Copyright © 1969-2003, Christian Literature International, P.O.Box 777 Canby, Oregon 97013

Design Director: Bill Johnson
Cover design by Justin Evans

Library of Congress Control Number: 2009935578
International Standard Book Number: 978-1-59979-946-9
First Edition
09 10 11 12 13 — 9 8 7 6 5 4 3 2 1
Printed in the United States of America

♥

I dedicate this book to my Big-Hearted wife, Ruth. Through unconditional love, patience, kindness, and grace, she has stayed near to me through the ebb and flow of life. She is my best friend, closest companion, wisest confidant, and the love of my life.

CONTENTS

PREFACE

The dawn of the new millennium was still fresh in the memory of the global community. Weeks before, concerns about the Y2K computer meltdown fizzled like the falling sparks from the fireworks that introduced the New Year. The first quarter of the year 2000 was almost past. It was during this time that I began to feel my heart stirred to share something sadly underreported in our modern era. I'm referring to the recognition of a special group of people, members of the human race with many differences and even obvious flaws, yet similar in one common trait—they are all Big-Hearted People. "Making a difference in people's lives, no matter the cost" is their mission statement. "Do unto others as you would have them do unto you" is their core value.

Their kind actions and contributions often go unnoticed and unrecognized, except from the recipients. You rarely see the media reporting about their Big-Heartedness unless it's considered significant and newsworthy. Yet, publicity is not what motivates Big-Hearted People; they just see a need and meet it, regardless. They don't feel compelled to wave a flag to draw attention to themselves or advertise their generosity. They simply treat others as they would have others treat them.

I have personally seen and experienced the wonderful results of Big-Heartedness through what some consider seemingly small and insignificant acts, and because of it I'm shouting from the housetops. My goal is not to promote volunteerism (though I believe it's valuable) or to suggest getting hyper-busy performing good deeds because it's "what we should be doing." But rather, promoting Big-Heartedness as a way of life, something that just comes naturally.

I have approached the subject of Big-Heartedness with a threefold purpose: first, describing Big-Hearted People and their shared attributes; second, defining guiding principles that enable Big-Hearted People to effectively reach out to others with hope and healing; third, encouraging those who think that what they do for others seems small and insignificant. The concepts in the succeeding chapters are not revolutionary or anything new. In all honesty, they're relatively simple. Perhaps some of it you've heard before.

I do not consider this book to be an all-inclusive, definitive guide to Big-Heartedness. Neither am I trying to promote some Big-Hearted idealism reached by only a privileged few. Rather, my intent is to provide a practical means to discover our God-given gifts, evaluate our inner motives, and tune our hearts to discern God's will. Realize that you and I are works in progress and don't need to become better before we can live a life of Big-Heartedness. God can use us just as we are and right where we are. You'll see this mentioned often throughout this book.

> For it is God who works in you both to will and to do for His good
> pleasure.
> —PHILIPPIANS 2:13, NKJV

A recurring theme I've highlighted throughout specific chapters is our need to experience an intimate, personal relationship with God. This is foundational. You will begin to see this come together and take shape as you read further. My prayer is that the eyes of your understanding will become enlightened to see just how much God wants to fellowship with you. You may even find the need to change your "religious" thinking to "relationship" thinking.

Where appropriate, I use poetry to emphasize, and in some cases summarize, some of the attributes or principles in the following chapters. My reasoning stems from the knowledge that poetry (like music), with its rhythm and meter, makes it easy to remember or memorize things we consider especially important. Take the time to read them in earnest with these thoughts in mind. In addition, I have created a companion study guide which may be downloaded for *free* at my Web site, www.bigheartedpeople.com. Since people on average only retain 10 percent of what they read, I have designed this study guide to help you increase your learning retention. I encourage you to take the time to answer the questions. You will find all the answers in the book.

You may notice the frequent use of the word *choice*. This is not merely coincidence. Our lives are comprised of choices—good and bad. The result of our choices either fills us with happiness and blessings or leaves us unsatisfied, and our lives lacking meaning. Therefore, I've sought to encourage you to use God's Word to make the right choices.

Echoing in my spirit are the verses of the anonymous psalmist in the acrostic Psalm 119. He declared, "Your word is a lamp to my feet and a light for my path" (Ps. 119:105, NIV). God's Word forms the foundation of everything I share with you. Please read the Scripture references in this book slowly and prayerfully. My sincere hope is that they will speak to you and you'll begin to look at Big-Heartedness in a new and exciting way. It is the power of His Word that will positively influence your life and overflow into people's lives, not my words.

Everything I'll share with you originates from a Judeo-Christian perspective. I cannot do otherwise without compromising my message. I have sought to transcend denominational barriers by providing a common connection and unity of purpose with God and fellow human beings. Big-Heartedness knows no boundaries.

The words nestled among these pages came about over years of biblical studies, careful observation, and personal experiences (both positive and negative). I have approached this wanting only to be a scribe and write as the Holy Spirit spoke to my spirit. I discovered the attributes and guiding principles that I highlight are just as necessary for me as for anyone. It has proven to be an incredible learning experience.

Imagine the time spent between these pages as though you were embarking on an exciting journey, one that takes you from a life of quantity to a life of quality—from trying to live a life of purpose, to discovering God's Big-Hearted purpose for your life.

ACKNOWLEDGMENTS

My deepest gratitude to the following Big-Hearted People, who unselfishly helped me transition this book from a gentle impression on my spirit to a concept—from a dream to a reality.

- To my daughters Amy, Leah, and Christa, Bob and Lois, Jim and Linda, Ron, Dr. Diane, and Drs. Jan and Caroline, whose insights and objective critiques were more valuable than they may have realized
- To Veanie, who faithfully agreed with me in prayer, knowing that with God all things are possible
- To authors Chris and Eric, whose advice and inspiration provided me with tremendous encouragement
- To Dr. Roy for his technical contribution

BIG-HEARTED PEOPLE

Big-Hearted People,
    overflowing with kindness.
Those who give themselves away
    abundantly; to you—to others.

Seeming to possess a special sense,
    as if they already know your deepest need;
       they'll do whatever it takes
to bless you at just the right time,
    in the most significant,
       generous way.

They're salt-of-the-earth folks,
    willing to get down with you
on hands and knees
      at ground level,
    bearing the heat of the day,
intermingling their life with yours.

Genuine smiles,
      hands reaching out,
    hugging you with their eyes;
It's easy to see their *Big Hearts*
    because they are so transparent.
      Enriching your life,
    they ask for nothing in return,
      except, that by your enrichment
you become a *Big-Hearted*
    person to someone else.

—R. J. SCHUM
MARCH 1, 2000

INTRODUCTION
Making a Difference

"I'm sorry, but there is no known cure. Medication can offer some relief, but you'll need to change your lifestyle—drastically." The doctor continued, "It's commonly known as fibromyalgia. The good news is that it won't kill you. The bad news is that you'll probably have to live with it the rest of your life."

The rheumatologist had just diagnosed the chronic pain and fatigue syndrome that had plagued me for over a decade. His words resonated in my mind as I tried to understand the implications of his revelation.

Years before, I noticed telltale symptoms, but they were minor. So, I just ignored them. During that time, I was engaged in charitable activities at church and elsewhere. Overall, I enjoyed good health and didn't let anything get me down. I was even performing freelance artwork besides working at my full-time job. My family was growing and prospering. Life was good. Yet the pain and fatigue steadily grew worse. Though I looked good on the outside, my internal health was taking a nosedive—fast. I needed more sleep to function normally. Alternative foods and eating habits became a necessity, not a choice. I saw different specialists and tried numerous medications, but none provided answers or the hope of relief.

It wasn't until the rheumatologist diagnosed my condition that I began to understand what I faced. I realized the need to reevaluate my commitments and change my lifestyle. It was already tough trying to get through a forty-hour workweek. I realized that I had to make some hard personal decisions—reducing or altogether eliminating many activities, even Big-Hearted ones, or so I thought.

Through circumstances that began to shape my life, I realized that Big-Heartedness was not what I previously imagined. Performing notable deeds, ministering to the needy masses, or volunteering at every opportunity might just not be what makes up Big-Heartedness. Maybe all I needed to do was simply use my God-given gifts, no matter how small, to bless others. At the time, it was all I could do.

I soon discovered that a simple phone call or encouraging greeting card could lift a person's spirit. I found that a brief, heartfelt prayer and gentle hug could relieve someone's burdens. The evidence stared me in the face. I saw that the simple, ordinary things I did for people had a more far-reaching impact than I realized.

Around this time, the subject of people with big hearts came up in a conversation with my friend Donna. Her husband, Doug, was someone I worked with for several years. He and I developed a friendship because we owned motorcycles and shared a common enjoyment of riding. Though some would consider Doug a bit rough around the edges, he was one of those people who you could always count on to do what is right. Thoughtful, honest, and always going out of his way to help other people even at the expense of personal comfort was the hallmark of his character. I commented to Donna that I considered Doug to be a Big-Hearted Person. I shared how I felt inspired to write a poem about him and others I knew who displayed Big-Hearted attributes.

After completing the poem, I mailed it to Doug and Donna and to my uncle, another Big-Hearted Person, as a tribute. During the span of almost a decade, the Lord used this poem to teach me about the importance of Big-Heartedness. He has also used it to inspire Big-Heartedness in others and recognize those who make a difference in people's lives—no matter how small their contributions seem.

But, what *really* makes someone Big-Hearted? What sets them apart from others—specifically from the self-focused populace who live life only for themselves? In your search to discover the answers, maybe the first step begins by me asking *you* a question.

ENTER THE BIG-HEARTED

When you hear about someone admired as having a big heart, what picture comes to mind?

Perhaps it's someone with a ready smile who is willing to help anyone in need, regardless of the cost. Maybe you imagine a person who serves others unselfishly, enabling them to live life in all its fullness. Possibly, it could be an individual who sees value in everyone and treats people with love and compassion.

Well, if you're like me, you see them possessing those same qualities too, and so much more. Simply stated, Big-Hearted People are just *ordinary* people with an *extraordinary* desire to bless others.

I can think of many wonderful Big-Hearted People I've met along the way and some I've known well for a long time. It warms my heart and puts a smile on my face when they come to mind—special people who have sown good things into my life. They have always been there to love me unconditionally and help me through some of my most difficult times. They saw my potential and encouraged me to look beyond what I could see with my eyes—into the realm of faith and possibility. It's because of them and God's grace that I have achieved what I never imagined possible. These Big-Hearted People became the greatest influences in my life.

I readily think of two couples, Jerry and Shirley and Doug and Mary, who showed acceptance, love, and kindness to me when I was a headstrong, rebellious teenager. Their Big-Heartedness enabled me to change my life's direction. There was Walter, a master

> Big-Hearted People are just *ordinary* people with an *extraordinary* desire to bless others.

calligrapher, who mentored me for many years in the lettering arts and manuscript illumination. He never asked anything from me, except to share the same passion for the art of beautiful writing.

However, there are kind souls who blessed me in ways that some people would consider insignificant, yet they inspired my life greatly. A greeting card sent from a friend who told me how much they loved and appreciated me when I needed it most. A phone call from a kindred spirit who sensed I was in need of comfort and encouragement. I vividly remember how generous friends from our church brought home-cooked meals to us when my wife was in the hospital. There also were those who blessed us financially during times of unemployment.

You probably know Big-Hearted People who made a difference in your life as well, or maybe you are a Big-Hearted Person making a difference in the lives of others; and if so, I wholeheartedly salute you!

The truth is, it doesn't take a college education, great wisdom, or even extraordinary abilities to be a Big-Hearted Person. William Wordsworth so eloquently wrote in his lines composed "a few miles above" Tintern Abbey, "That best portion of a good man's life, His little, nameless, unremembered acts of kindness and love."[1]

CREATING THE GOOD

If only we would take a moment to reflect on life and ask ourselves, What's life all about, and why are we here on this little planet? Is it just about how many possessions we can amass and personal pleasures fulfill? If that were the sum total of our existence, life would be so empty. God created us not only to obtain fulfillment from receiving but, even more, from giving. Some people constantly seek self-gratification, because they think it satisfies, but find the more they fill themselves, the emptier their lives become. What a sobering dilemma this reveals. Continuously poured into like the Dead Sea but never pouring out, they become reservoirs instead of channels.

The truth is, it doesn't take a college education, great wisdom, or even extraordinary abilities to be a Big-Hearted Person.

Helen Keller once said, "Many persons have a wrong idea of what constitutes true happiness. It is not attained through self-gratification but through fidelity to a worthy purpose."[2] Personally, I can't think of a more worthy purpose than being Big-Hearted to my fellow human beings. In retrospect, when I think about the former years of my life, I can truthfully say the most memorable events were times when I gave to others. Surprisingly, some would consider most of what I did to be little and simple at best. Yet it made a difference when sowed into the lives of others. Maybe you've seen people blessed because of your Big-Heartedness, and if so, you know exactly what I mean.

God grants gifts to each of us that we can use for the good of mankind, regardless of our situation in life. It is up to us to ask for His guidance and enabling to fulfill this awesome and wonderful commission. Winston Churchill simply but wisely stated, "We make a living by what we get, but we make a life by what we give."[3] What we get may only offer us temporary pleasure, but what we give has the capacity to live forever. Of course, our motives shouldn't be to give just to receive. However, there exists an immutable law that God established, known as the law of reciprocity. It works simply by giving. Jesus confirmed this principle by saying, "Give, and it will be given to you. You will have more than enough. It can be pushed down and shaken together and it will still run over as it is given to you. The way you give to others is the way you will receive in return" (Luke 6:38, NEW LIFE). If you give love, you will receive love; if you sow kindness, you will reap kindness; if you show compassion, you will receive compassion. Do you see this? Think about what a major impact we could make in this world for good if we understood and practiced this principle.

MANKIND IS OUR BUSINESS

Most of us are familiar with the classic novel *A Christmas Carol* by Charles Dickens. Jacob Marley's ghost speaks one of the most moving statements in this story while grieving because of life's misused opportunities. Scrooge, with faltering speech, begins to identify with Marley's regret and says, "But you were always a good man of business, Jacob." Upon hearing his words, the tormented ghost cries out, "Business! Mankind was my business. The common welfare was my business; charity, mercy, forbearance, and benevolence were all my business. The dealings of my trade were but a drop of water in the comprehensive ocean of my business!"[4]

Who are the people who mobilize to help and offer aid in the aftermath of natural disasters? Big-Hearted People! Who are the first individuals to show compassion and love to those suffering from a personal tragedy? Big-Hearted People! Who are the selfless ones providing hope and comfort to those with desperate needs regardless of societal status? Big-Hearted People! These are the kind souls who often ask, "How are you?" with genuine concern. Why? Because they're just looking for an opportunity to do good for someone.

I realize that not everyone naturally shows Big-Heartedness. It's obvious; just watch the evening news. It's also evident that some people do possess a natural tendency to help others. Nevertheless, each of us has the capacity to love and act with Big-Heartedness. I'm not a naturally Big-Hearted Person but rather quite selfish. However, through heart-changing experiences that started with a personal relationship with Jesus Christ, I began to view life differently. Now, I'm not where I want to be—yet; but thankfully I'm not what I used to be. As I exercise Big-Heartedness, I find that it's progressively becoming a part of my nature. I want to be someone who sows good things into people's lives instead of taking something from them. Do you know people who just drain the energy from you when you're with them? You leave feeling emotionally and sometimes even physically exhausted.

Maybe you don't show Big-Heartedness as often as you would like. Well there's good news for you, my friend. I believe you can experience a change of heart. First, make the deliberate decision to become Big-Hearted. Second, pray that God will give you the grace and wisdom

> What we *get* may only offer us temporary pleasure, but what we *give* has the capacity to live forever.

to make a difference in people's lives. Third, put it into practice—right now. Once you do this, you will begin to see opportunities unfold at work, at school, in your neighborhood, in your church, or wherever your footsteps take you. Find out what people need and help to meet it. The more you perform Big-Heartedness, the more the desire will grow in you, especially when you see lives changed.

BEARING THE FRUITS OF BIG-HEARTEDNESS

Big-Hearted People are givers. They have found that it's, indeed, more blessed to give than to receive. However, I would be to blame if I didn't mention that being a Big-Hearted Person often takes sacrifice—sometimes small, sometimes great. You may have to sacrifice your personal time or finances, and even your own comfort. It may require you to forego buying something you really wanted so another can buy basic necessities. It may require you to sacrifice your own dreams to help others obtain theirs. I firmly believe this is the reason it results in such a great blessing to the recipient. Would it be as valuable if it cost us nothing? Big-Hearted People have also learned to serve. In our modern society, there's so much talk about being served but little talk about how to serve. Some may think that serving is degrading or strictly for those without a "proper" education. Nothing can be further from the truth!

Most of us are familiar with the life of Mother Teresa, who selflessly served the impoverished, destitute, and outcasts. She did not care to receive special recognition for the kindness she showed. Yet, look at how greatly she influenced so many people. Some considered her a saint. Why? It wasn't because of her education or cultural status but because she knew how to serve—in love. She humbly stated, "I do not pray for success; I ask for faithfulness."[5] Don't her words seem distant and out of place in our success-driven society?

In our modern society, there's so much talk about being served but little talk about how to serve.

The greatest leaders are those who first learned to serve. Without exception, the greatest person who ever lived was the Lord Jesus Christ, and He declared that He came not to be served but to serve. Shouldn't we desire the same? There are many other examples of those who gave a lifetime of service, and it only started with one act—an act of Big-Heartedness.

Is the sum total of our Christian experience attending church, reading our Bibles, and praying? If so, we might have missed an important Christian responsibility—to encourage, strengthen, and bless whomever God places in the pathway of our lives. Did He give us unique gifts to use them only for ourselves or just to be busy doing "church work"? If you search the writings of the apostles in Scripture, you will find the real answer.

Rejoice with those who rejoice [sharing others' joy], and weep with those who weep [sharing others' grief]. Live in harmony with one another; do not be haughty (snobbish, high-minded, exclusive), but readily adjust yourself to [people, things] and give yourselves to humble tasks. Never overestimate yourself or be wise in your own conceits.

—ROMANS 12:15–16, AMP

Stay on good terms with each other, held together by love. Be ready with a meal or a bed when it is needed. Why, some have extended hospitality to angels without ever knowing it! Regard prisoners as if you were in prison with them. Look on victims of abuse as if what happened to them had happened to you.

—HEBREWS 13:1–3, THE MESSAGE

Anyone who sets himself up as "religious" by talking a good game is self-deceived. This kind of religion is hot air and only hot air. Real religion, the kind that passes muster before God the Father, is this: Reach out to the homeless and loveless in their plight, and guard against corruption from the godless world.

—JAMES 1:26–27, THE MESSAGE

Big-Hearted People are not perfect people. Big-Hearted People just have an overwhelming desire to make a difference in the lives of others! Consider the wisdom of nineteenth-century Quaker Stephen Grellet, who penned these words: "I expect to pass through this world but once. Any good thing, therefore, that I can do, or any kindness I can show a fellow being, let me do it now. Let me not defer or neglect it, for I shall not pass this way again."[6]

I find it fitting to end this introduction with a scripture containing a wonderful promise to those who show Big-Heartedness.

And if you give what you have to the hungry, and fill the needs of those who suffer, then your light will rise in the darkness, and your darkness will be like the brightest time of day. The Lord will always lead you. He will meet the needs of your soul in the dry times and give strength to your body. You will be like a garden that has enough water, like a well of water that never dries up.

—ISAIAH 58:10–11, NEW LIFE

Let these truths be the inspiration for us to live as Big-Hearted People and overflow with kindness.

MAKE A DIFFERENCE

Like saplings planted in the earth,
With want of leaves and buds to show,
For to survive they now must strive,
And flourish where they grow.

So we should then bloom where planted,
And make a difference with our lives,
For what we need to bless others,
Within our heart abides.

Make a difference and take a stand,
In your city or town or school,
Make a difference, give truth a voice,
Let liberty ensue.

Make a difference in your country,
Keep freedom's radiant flame alive,
Make a difference in your marriage,
That love may grow and thrive.

Make a difference where you work, and
Inspire others to do their best,
Make a difference in your family,
Be first to serve the rest.

Make a difference in a child's life,
Be a mentor, inspire and teach,
Make a difference in your church, and
Help hope extend its reach.

Make a difference to the outcast,
And give them worth and dignity,
Make a difference, reach out to those,
Hurt by calamity.

If everyone made an effort,
To show love in the simplest way,
People's lives would be much better,
By making someone's day.

So whether you may find yourself,
In the most pleasant place or not,
Just make a difference where you are,
By using what you've got.

—R. J. Schum

Part I

SEVEN ATTRIBUTES OF BIG-HEARTED PEOPLE

During years of personal experiences and careful observation, I have noticed seven specific attributes that embody Big-Hearted People. They are:

1. kindness
2. empathy
3. compassion
4. self-sacrifice
5. selfless giving
6. unconditional love
7. sensitivity to people's needs

In the following chapters, I'll explain how and why these attributes are significant. However, before I do, I want to share something again that I consider extremely important. Big-Hearted People are not perfect people. Big-Hearted People just have an overwhelming desire to make a difference in the lives of others. They are just as apt to make mistakes, fail, and—I'll use the *s* word here—sin.

All of us are imperfect. Who among us may boast otherwise? I believe it all boils down to our heart's motives, what drives us. Do we want to be a blessing and an instrument of God's loving-kindness and compassion? If so, our heart will not condemn us if we occasionally stumble. (If you would like a further explanation, stop now, bookmark this page, and read chapter 17, "Imperfectly Perfect.")

Will all these attributes be present every time we show Big-Heartedness? It's possible, but more likely each one will reveal itself in opportunities when we allow God to bless people through us. On occasion, we will show forth these graces naturally, without even thinking. At other times, we will need to make a determined decision to act with Big-Heartedness. Let's ask ourselves, How can I look at others with a heart of compassion, or how can I show kindness today? Sometimes all it takes is just to change our mind-set to a "heart-set"—making it move from our heads to our hearts.

> Let's ask ourselves, How can I look at others with a heart of compassion, or how can I show kindness today?

As mentioned previously, God endows each of us with gifts that we can discover and use for His glory. Our unique-to-us gifts work together with these seven attributes to show Big-Heartedness to people whom God places in our path. For instance, two of my natural gifts are exhortation and encouragement. Most likely, they were the motivation for writing this book and founding the www.bigheartedpeople.com Web site. I also have gifts in music, art, and poetry. I have used some of these together on various occasions to show kindness to people who desperately needed words of comfort and healing.

What are your gifts? Perhaps you already know, or maybe some still need to be discovered. Either way, let nothing prevent you from using your gifts to be a Big-Hearted Person. Make a difference in the lives of others, and you will find yourself blessed as well!

Now, don't think that it's now your sole responsibility to solve world hunger or achieve world peace on your own. Your responsibility is to discover and apply your God-given gifts through Big-Heartedness. When you do, you'll understand and live the Big-Hearted purpose for your life. Allow God to use you where you are and with what you have. The apostle Paul, in his letter to the Romans, describes this with careful detail.

> So since we find ourselves fashioned into all these excellently formed and marvelously functioning parts in Christ's body, let's just go ahead and be what we were made to be, without enviously or pridefully comparing ourselves with each other, or trying to be something we aren't. If you preach, just preach God's Message, nothing else; if you help, just help, don't take over; if you teach, stick to your teaching; if you give encouraging guidance, be careful that you don't get bossy; if you're put in charge, don't manipulate; if you're called to give aid to people in distress, keep your eyes open and be quick to respond; if you work with the disadvantaged, don't let yourself get irritated with them or depressed by them. Keep a smile on your face.
>
> —ROMANS 12:5–8, THE MESSAGE

Greatness doesn't always come by achieving what some consider great things or performing deeds of largesse, but rather by showing love and kindness in small and simple ways. Horace Mann, nineteenth-century educator and politician, wrote these words of exhortation: "Doing nothing for others is the undoing of one's self. We must be purposely kind and generous, or we miss the best part of existence. The heart that goes out of itself, gets large and full of joy. This is the great secret of the inner life. We do ourselves the most good doing something for others."[1] This is an ideal quote to prepare us to examine these seven attributes as revealed in God's Word.

1

KINDNESS

Constant kindness can accomplish much. As the sun makes ice melt,
kindness causes misunderstanding, mistrust, and hostility to evaporate.

—ALBERT SCHWEITZER[1]

The collective voices of humanity desperately cry out for people whose lives express the virtue of kindness. News stories abound describing incidents of road rage, child and elder abuse, character assassinations, mean-spirited people, animal cruelty, and the list continues. As a result, even when we perform a small kindness on someone's behalf, it is still most welcome. Kindness is like a momentary oasis where we can revel in a benevolence performed by another human being to encourage, strengthen, comfort, or meet a need. It may come in the form of words, money, a special favor, tangible gift, or just a simple touch or smile. Kindness always looks for opportunities of expression, even in simple ways, because it knows the power of its value to the recipient.

In the book of Galatians, the Apostle Paul describes the nine fruits of the Spirit, one of which is kindness (also translated gentleness). Each of these fruits represents certain characteristics of God's nature. They become a part of our spiritual nature too as we resist the passions of our carnal nature, abide in Jesus Christ, and allow the Holy Spirit to help us. A biblical term that accurately describes the kindness that God lavishes upon us is loving-kindness. A simple definition is "tender and benevolent affection." Romans 12:10 states: "Be kindly affectionate to one another with brotherly love, in honor giving preference to one another" (NKJV). God expresses His kindness to others through us as we allow Him.

WHO IS MY NEIGHBOR?

The story of the *Good Samaritan* is a timeless example of loving-kindness in action. The Apostle Luke describes Jesus' response to a question by a religion scholar (religious leader) who asked, "Who is my neighbor?" Jesus answered by telling a parable about a man who journeyed from Jerusalem to Jericho. As he traveled, robbers attacked him, stole his clothing, beat him, and left him half-dead.

> Luckily, a priest was on his way down the same road, but when he saw him he angled across to the other side. *Then a Levite religious man showed up; he also avoided the injured man.*
>
> *Next*, a Samaritan traveling along the road came on him. When he saw the man's [*pitiful*] condition, his heart went out to him [*moved with compassion*]. He gave him first aid, disinfecting and bandaging his wounds. Then he lifted him onto his donkey, led him to an inn, and made him comfortable. In the morning he took out two silver coins and gave them to the innkeeper, saying, "Take good care of him. If it costs any more, put it on my bill—I'll pay you on my way back."
>
> *Jesus, looking through the religion scholar's bodily presence, and deep into his soul asked him*: "What do you think? Which of the three became a neighbor to the man attacked by robbers?" "The one who treated him kindly," the religion scholar responded. (*Since Jesus already knew how he would answer, He targeted his hard heart.*) Jesus said, "Go and do the same."
>
> —LUKE 10:31, 34–37, THE MESSAGE

A priest and Levite avoided the injured man. No doubt, they had very important things to do, like religious matters, which of course, should be top priority, right? *No!* We can be busy performing *religious* duties and still not be fulfilling God's purpose for our lives. He doesn't call us to be "busy" but to bear fruit for His glory. Often, we produce fruit by showing simple kindnesses to people during everyday life. According to Jesus' parable, showing kindness *is* doing the "will of God," or as He stated earlier, "loving your neighbor as well as you love yourself."

The origin of the Samaritans makes an interesting study. History describes their ancient heritage as originating from both Jews and Assyrians. During Jesus' time, the Jewish people despised them. In this parable, Jesus (himself being a Jew) was pointing out that all people are worthy of compassion and kindness regardless of their ethnic origin. God created mankind in His image, not a physical, but a spiritual image because He is Spirit. He doesn't look on our outward appearance but only on our heart, which is the same as our spirit. "God judges persons differently than humans do. Men and women look at the face; God looks into the heart" (1 Sam. 16:7, THE MESSAGE). He asks us to view our fellow creatures the same.

THE BISHOP AND THE THIEF

Let's fast-forward about 1,800 years to the time of the French revolution. The author Victor Hugo, in his wonderful story of redemption and forgiveness, *Les Misérables,* describes the life of one man, Jean Valjean. (If you haven't read the book or seen any of the movies, find the time to do so. You'll enjoy it.) He spent nineteen hard years in prison and galleys. His only crimes were stealing a loaf of bread (to feed his widowed sister and her seven children) and several attempts to escape from prison. Eventually released into society—but with papers that identify him as a former convict—he finds that nobody will offer him a meal. Even children pelt him with stones. Valjean can't escape his past, and people view him as nothing more than a despised outcast.

After traveling to the town of Digne, he looks for lodging or shelter for the night, but everyone refuses him—time after time. The only welcome he receives is from Monsignor Bienvenu, the godly bishop (*bienvenue* means "welcome" in French) who feeds Jean and offers him a room with a bed. Valjean accepts his host's hospitality

> Kindness always looks for opportunities of expression, even in simple ways, because it knows the power of its value to the recipient.

but does not repay him likewise. In the early morning hours, he steals the bishop's silverware and flees into the darkness. Let's follow this narrative as it unfolds at the bishop's residence.

> Just as the brother [Monseigneur Bienvenu] and [his] sister [Madame Magloire] were rising from the table, there was a knock at the door. "Come in," said the bishop.
>
> The door opened. A strange, fierce group appeared on the threshold. Three men were holding a fourth by the collar. The three men were gendarmes; the fourth Jean Valjean. A brigadier of gendarmes, who appeared to head the group, was near the door. He advanced towards the bishop, giving a military salute. "Monseigneur," said he—

At this word Jean Valjean, who was sullen and seemed entirely cast down, raised his head with a stupefied air—

"Monseigneur!" he murmured, "then it is not the curé [not just a parish priest but a bishop]!"

"Silence!" said a gendarme, "it is monseigneur, the bishop." In the meantime Monseigneur Bienvenu had approached as quickly as his great age permitted: "Ah, there you are," said he, looking towards Jean Valjean. "I am glad to see you. But! I gave you the candlesticks also, which are silver like the rest, and would bring two hundred francs. Why did you not take them along with your plates?" Jean Valjean opened his eyes and looked at the bishop with an expression which no human tongue could describe.

"Monseigneur," said the brigadier, "then what this man said was true? We met him. He was going like a man who was running away, and we arrested him in order to see. He had this silver." "And he told you," interrupted the bishop, with a smile, "that it had been given him by a good old priest with whom he had passed the night. I see it all. And you brought him back here? It is all a mistake." "If that is so," said the brigadier, "we can let him go." "Certainly," replied the bishop. The gendarmes released Jean Valjean, who shrank back—

"Is it true that they let me go?" he said in a voice almost inarticulate, as if he were speaking in his sleep. "Yes! you can go. Do you not understand?" said a gendarme. [Please notice how the bishop now addresses Jean Valjean.] "My friend," said the bishop, "before you go away, here are your candlesticks; take them." He went to the mantelpiece, took the two candlesticks, and brought them to Jean Valjean. The two women beheld the action without a word, or gesture, or look, that might disturb the bishop. Jean Valjean was trembling in every limb. He took the two candlesticks mechanically, and with a wild appearance. "Now," said the Bishop, "go in peace. By the way, my friend, when you come again, you need not come through the garden. You can always come in and go out by the front door. It is closed only with a latch, day or night." Then turning to the gendarmes, he said: "Messieurs, you can retire." The gendarmes withdrew. Jean Valjean felt like a man who is just about to faint. The bishop approached him, and said, in a low voice: "Forget not, never forget that you have promised me to use this silver to become an honest man." Jean Valjean, who had no recollection of this promise, stood confounded. The bishop had laid much stress upon these words as he uttered them.

He continued, solemnly: [This scene brings tears to my eyes as the bishop now addresses Jean Valjean as "brother" and speaks these words with love, yet with great spiritual authority.] "Jean Valjean, my brother: you belong no longer to evil, but to good. It is your soul that I am buying for you. I withdraw it from dark thoughts and from the spirit of perdition, and I give it to God!"[2]

Those words changed Jean Valjean forever. He accepted God's forgiveness through this humble bishop. Valjean changed from a thief to an honest, upright person. Eventually he changes his name, settles in the small town of Montreuil, and becomes a wealthy businessman and the town's mayor. The remaining story describes incidents with many people to whom he showed kindness. He reached out to the impoverished and victims of social injustice. He provided shelter for those in need just like the saintly bishop did for him. However, through all this the obsessive, law-driven Inspector Javert relentlessly pursued him because of a parole violation. Nevertheless, Valjean still showed kindness and forgiveness to him despite opportunities to kill Javert.

> We can be busy performing *religious* duties and still not be fulfilling God's purpose for our lives.

One selfless act of loving-kindness by a godly bishop made the difference in the life of an unworthy soul shunned by society. Monsignor Bienvenu took an incredible risk by showing indiscriminate generosity to Jean Valjean. Yet, many other broken and desperate souls received kindness through the life of a redeemed convict. Sometimes we see kindness shown in dramatic ways as in the life of Monsignor Bienvenu; or sometimes an even smaller act produces a great benefit in someone's life. Allow me to share this personal story with you.

A BEAUTIFUL, WONDERFUL GIFT

The subject in the e-mail that just arrived read, "A Beautiful, Wonderful Gift." At first glance, I suspected that it might be some spam that much too often invades my e-mail inbox. Since there was no recent occasion where I was expecting a gift, it was highly suspect. No doubt it was an advertising ploy to get me to buy something I probably didn't need—or so I thought. Looking more carefully, I noticed the sender's e-mail address was someone with whom

I had just started to correspond. He was a fellow Christian and musician who sold a musical instrument to me.

Aaron (fictitious name) was someone whom I wish I had met in person instead of just by e-mail. Even through correspondence, it's often easy to determine what a person might be like on the inside. By what I read from this e-mail, I knew he was a kindred spirit. Those of you involved in the "arts" know exactly what I mean. He was receiving chemotherapy treatment, and although a positive individual, he seemed anxious. I had sensed this in earlier correspondence. A few days before receiving his e-mail, I had addressed an envelope using calligraphy and enclosed a greeting card. In the card, I wrote an encouraging personal message hoping it would uplift his spirit.

The text of his resulting e-mail read exactly as follows:

> Hi Randy,
>
> I have to tell you about the most beautiful, wonderful gift that a wonderful person sent to me…a beautiful, wonderful card with the most wonderful thoughts of encouragement and an absolutely God-given talent for calligraphy. THANK YOU, RANDY! You had no idea how much that lifted my spirits…the thoughts and the time it took to write so eloquently and that someone cared so much to do that. You are truly a wonderful person! I was so lifted by it and timed so perfectly 'cause I received it during the roughest part of chemo. I had no doubt that your thoughts and prayers throughout had a major impact on my outcome.
>
> Chemo is over and I have radiation to look forward to. Chemo was okay at first but got progressively worse but even so, the doctors said that I did not even look like someone going through chemo…no hair loss and blood counts are all normal during it and I have even gone bicycling when I feel up to it. Just had another PET/CT scan and came back "100% pristine." Still have to go through radiation though just to make sure any stray cancer cells are killed off. Well, I am about halfway there.

He then went on to tell me about some of the arts activities that occupied his time.

> …Thank you so much again for the very thoughtful and uplifting card…amazing! May God bless you. I must say I certainly believe

you had a big hand in my recovery and I'll never forget that. I hope you are doing very well and that God is blessing you and your family with much wealth and happiness, you certainly deserve it.

Your friend,

Aaron

I share this testimony not to draw attention to me for it was strictly the grace of God working through me to bless someone else. I had no idea my card would have such a major impact on my friend. I just did it because it was stirring in my spirit. I simply took a few minutes of my time and wrote a personal message; the outcome was incredibly powerful. It helped me to see how important it is to show simple kindnesses to others and to do it without hesitation—because timing can mean everything.

So often, we think that these gentle, prompting thoughts in our minds are just random and we quickly dismiss them. I have found the opposite to be true. This highlights one way God speaks to us, so we should always listen for His leading and be ready to obey Him. In chapter 7 I expound on how we can discern God's voice. These words penned by Ralph Waldo Emerson give a sense of urgency and are so suitable to close this chapter: "You cannot do a kindness too soon, for you never know how soon it will be too late."[3]

2

EMPATHY

There is much satisfaction in work well done; praise is sweet; but there can be no happiness equal to the joy of finding a heart that understands.[1]

—Victor Robinsoll

Several years ago because of chronic pain, my doctor prescribed medication that helped me sleep through the night. Through a misunderstanding of the potential side effects, I became dependent; or in another term that some don't like to use, *addicted*. It was a horrible experience and one I wouldn't wish on anyone. My doctor offered advice about how to wean myself from these drugs and graciously supported me. But each time I tried his recommendations, the withdrawal symptoms grew worse.

I was at my wit's end and had no idea how to come off these medications without horrendous side effects. On one Sunday morning during church, I came forward and asked my brothers and sisters in Christ to pray for me. A good friend, John, led the congregation in prayer and asked the Lord to give me wisdom to find my pathway to healing.

After performing an Internet search during the following week, I found a forum that provided exactly what I needed. It was for people who experienced addiction from this same family of drugs. Some were in dire need and looking for advice; others were offering encouragement and support. I sent out a desperate e-mail hoping that someone could help me with my prescription drug problem. The result of my search was obviously no coincidence.

Because of my plea, I received three responses that offered me hope. Judith, a woman from North Carolina (now a close friend), a man from England, and another from Florida responded to my e-mail. Each gave me advice, and two agreed to pray for me regularly. This eventually led to an end to my dependence on this medication. After a withdrawal of 174 days, I was *free*, praise God!

Since these three kind souls experienced prescription drug addiction, they understood what I was going through and were able to help me. Since then, through empathy, I have prayed for and supported others with addictions similar to mine because I also "walked the same road."

Empathy is defined as feeling, experiencing or understanding *someone else's* pain or suffering within *your heart* because you've become so aware (cognitively perceptive) and sensitive to another that you emotionally enter into their situation or condition (you place yourself into another's shoes) or you've already gone through the same thing.

This is precisely why support groups can help people. Those who suffer from grief, health problems, addictions, family distress, or abuse can meet with others who understand firsthand because:

- They have a friend or relative in the same situation.
- They share the same personal experience.

DO UNTO OTHERS—WITH EMPATHY

Many refer to Jesus' words in Luke 6:31, NIV, as the Golden Rule: "Do to others as you would have them do to you." Often, we don't immediately relate this scripture to empathy. However, if you carefully consider these words, you may realize that empathy is often the motivation for heeding them, particularly if you're a Big-Hearted Person.

If someone showed you love and compassion, especially when you didn't deserve it, you'd probably be quick to show it to others. If you experienced forgiveness for an offense or some great debt, no doubt, you'd forgive others of their transgressions against you as well.

The same holds true from the opposite perspective. If someone's careless words have hurt you, most likely, you wouldn't speak similarly to others. If people deceived you through dishonesty, you would certainly be truthful and ethical in your personal and business affairs. The negative, painful experiences you faced made you aware of what others would experience if you acted in like manner.

I believe that people who most show empathy have tender hearts. Through personal distress or tragedy, they became broken and their hearts softened. They look at someone's suffering or unfortunate condition and see themselves as once being there. Empathy compels them to reach out with understanding and offer whatever help is necessary.

DARK NIGHTS OF THE SOUL

Sometimes we don't understand why we experience difficult trials in our life and may even ask God why. We think nobody else is suffering like us and enduring similar hardships. Take heart, my friend; *God knows the depth of your suffering.* As you trust Him, He will lead you to someone who can identify with your struggles—one who can understand your heartaches. These Big-Hearted People will empathize with your suffering and help you along the pathway of recovery and wholeness. They will pray and stand with you until you receive victory over fiery trials that come your way. That is why God emphatically urges you in His Word to fellowship with like-minded Christian believers.

> Take heart, my friend; *God knows the depth of your suffering.* As you trust Him, He will lead you to someone who can identify with your struggles— one who can understand your heartaches.

Perhaps you sometimes wonder where God is when your life turns upside down—when you're rapidly approaching the end of your rope. Are the floodwaters rising higher and higher until it looks as if you will drown unless He rescues you? Does darkness seem to cover you like a blanket? There is One who is empathetic and who understands. He too had passions like us and received some of the worst physical and emotional pain this world could inflict. Jesus Christ, the man of sorrows—the One acquainted with grief. (See Isaiah 53.)

This is the distinctive characteristic of Christianity. God almighty in the person of Jesus Christ chose to come to the earth He created—to live among the human beings He created and share their experiences. Finally, He offered Himself as a sacrifice for the sins of mankind, giving life in exchange for death and joy in exchange for grief. God intimately understands rejection, criticism, abuse, and scorning. He knows what it's like to have weakness, pain, and temptation, and to experience deep sorrow. It's important to remember that Jesus did not save mankind through His miracles but by His suffering.

God did not only want to have pity for the human race, He also wanted to have empathy. He wanted to feel what we feel. The following verse from the book of Hebrews supports this.

> Now that we know what we have—Jesus, this great High Priest with ready access to God—let's not let it slip through our fingers. We

don't have a priest who is out of touch with our reality. He's been through weakness and testing, experienced it all—all but the sin.
—HEBREWS 4:14–15, THE MESSAGE

As humans, we naturally shun difficulty and suffering. We do whatever is necessary to remove it far from us. This understandably is a normal reaction, for who likes pain? However, if we commit ourselves to God and trust Him when we are "in the midst of the fire," He will turn it around for good. Through our personal experience, the truth of this scripture will become real: "And we know that all things work together for good to those who love God, to those who are the called according to *His* purpose" (Rom. 8:28, NKJV). Now it does not say everything turns out the way we want it to happen or according to our timetable. Allow me to paraphrase this verse for clarification: "And we know that everything in our lives God shapes together for His good purpose and plan; to bring Him glory and produce fruit in us, with eternal value."

I haven't enjoyed experiencing pain and heartache in my life. I didn't delight in the emotional distresses I faced during personal "dark (obscure) nights of the soul." Yet, I've discovered that sometimes in the darkest nights, the brightness of God's presence still breaks forth. I haven't relished the times when, by my own choice, I've fallen into sin and suffered the consequences.

> God did not only want to have pity for the human race, He also wanted to have empathy.

Nevertheless, in hindsight, I saw how God in His mercy brought forth much good through *all* these difficult experiences. Some were hard lessons and some caused heartache. But God has taught me (and is still teaching me) to trust Him, regardless. I'm now able to empathize with others suffering with similar problems, struggles, and even failures. Through it all, I have experienced the wonder of His love, forgiveness, and grace.

THE BONDS OF EMPATHY

A special bond forms when people know you've experienced similar afflictions. They are more trusting and apt to believe you more readily because of it. There are seasons in our lives where we will help and comfort others; but also, seasons where they will reach out and comfort us.

In the second of Paul's letter to the church in Corinth, he stresses this truth with simple practicality:

All praise to the God and Father of our Master, Jesus the Messiah!
Father of all mercy! God of all healing counsel! He comes alongside us when we go through hard times, and before you know it, he
brings us alongside someone else who is going through hard times
so that we can be there for that person just as God was there for us.
We have plenty of hard times that come from following the Messiah,
but no more so than the good times of his healing comfort—we get
a full measure of that, too.

When we suffer for Jesus, it works out for your healing and salvation. If we are treated well, given a helping hand and encouraging
word, that also works to your benefit, spurring you on, face forward,
unflinching. Your hard times are also our hard times. When we see
that you're just as willing to endure the hard times as to enjoy the
good times, we know you're going to make it, no doubt about it.

—2 CORINTHIANS 1:3–7, THE MESSAGE

During the Last Supper, Jesus spoke something of great importance to
Simon Peter. Although, at the time, Peter had no idea what Jesus was revealing.
"Simon, Simon, Satan has asked to sift you as wheat. But I have prayed for
you, Simon, that your faith may not fail. And when you have turned back,
strengthen your brothers" (Luke 22:31–32, NIV). Jesus previously changed
Simon's name to Peter, meaning "rock." Yet in this passage, He addresses him
as Simon. Why? Jesus knew Simon would deny Him three times, but was telling
him that although he would falter, his faith would not (this is because faith is
a force that brings us back to God). After Simon repented and turned back to
Jesus—after he learned about His love and forgiveness—Peter, the rock, could
strengthen others because of his experience.

Since the Lord is empathetic, He draws close to those with broken hearts.
"The LORD is close to the brokenhearted and saves those who are crushed in
spirit" (Ps. 34:18, NIV). So, as Big-Hearted People, we can be certain that the
Lord will lead us to hurting people. Often it's just to listen and let them know
we care—not providing solutions or dialoguing—but simply listening. There is
power in just allowing someone to open their hearts and share their afflictions.
However, our goal should be to lead them to Jesus upon whom they can cast
their care. "Casting the whole of your care [all your anxieties, all your worries,
all your concerns, once and for all] on Him, for He cares for you affection-
ately and cares about you watchfully" (1 Pet. 5:7, AMP). Jesus, the empathetic
One, who can heal their heartaches, meet their deepest needs, and satisfy the
longing of their souls.

3

COMPASSION

Of what avail is an open eye, if the heart is blind?[1]

—Solomon ibn Gabirol

*The purpose of human life is to serve and to show
compassion and the will to help others.*[2]

—Albert Schweitzer

Root Awakenings

The evolutions of word origins and meanings have always fascinated me. Years ago, I remember listening to poet and etymologist John Ciardi on the radio. He brought new life to familiar words by examining their roots, explaining their historical significance, and unearthing other literary "nuggets." These word treasures never ceased to captivate me. His familiar benediction, "good words to you," invariably announced the end of every discourse. Please allow me, though maybe with less finesse, to expound similarly on the attribute of compassion.

People often use the words *compassion*, *pity*, and *sympathy*, synonymously. Looking into their origins, one discovers a common thread of meaning, but at the same time, distinctive characteristics. This enables the interchanging of these words or the preferential use of one over another.

Sympathy stems from Latin and Greek roots dating from the sixteenth century. Its simplest definition is "having *similar* or common feelings." Taking the definition one step further, it means "the act or capacity of *entering into or sharing* the feelings of another."[3] Sometimes people use sympathy in place of empathy or conversely. However, when compared with empathy as defined in chapter 2, a distinct difference readily appears.

Pity dates from thirteenth century Anglo-French and Latin roots. Interestingly, it stems from the early words *piety* or *pious*, meaning "upright, dutiful, kind, and gracious." *Pity* eventually evolved into the modern definition of: "sympathetic sorrow for one suffering, distressed or unhappy."[4] The feeling of pity primarily comes when it considers the weak, troubled, or miserable condition of the object. In the Old Testament, *pity* derives from the Hebrew words:

- *chamal*: "to spare," similar to "mercy"[5]
- *racham*: "to love deeply, to be compassionate."[6]

Although *sympathy* and *pity* have subtle differences, we often find them used interchangeably.

Compassion finds its roots in fourteenth century Anglo-French and late Latin origins. Compassion is both pity, where the heart aches because of the suffering it sees, and sympathy, where it enters to share the feeling of the one who suffers. It also introduces a unique characteristic, which raises it to a higher level than sympathy or pity. Compassion wants to do something to relieve the suffering; it can't stand on the sidelines and merely observe. Someone may have pity and sympathy but not act on those feelings, but genuine compassion must do something about it. A detailed definition of this virtue is "a feeling of deep sympathy and [pity] sorrow for another who is stricken by misfortune, accompanied by a strong desire to alleviate the suffering."[7]

THE COMPASSIONATE HEART OF GOD

Throughout the Bible, the word *compassion* provides deep insight into God's compassionate heart. When we read examples of Jesus' compassion, the Greek root word used is *splagchnizomai* (just try to pronounce that!). This refers to being moved in the depths of the heart or "bowels." The bowels according to ancient thought were the seat of love and pity. This is clear in the words of the Apostle Paul in the King James translation of Colossians 3:12: "Put on therefore, as the elect of God, holy and beloved, bowels of mercies, kindness, humbleness of mind, meekness, longsuffering."

As described in chapter 1, the Good Samaritan's heart moved with pity when he saw the injured man and he acted with compassion. Loving-kindness flowed through him, and he did everything he could to relieve the man's suffering and get him back on his feet again.

The prodigal son is another well-known parable of Jesus that appears in the Gospel account of Luke. It is a story that beautifully depicts God's heart of compassion.

Jesus begins the parable by speaking about a man with two sons, one of which asked his father for his share of the estate. The father divided his property between them, and the older son received his share but remained at home. However, the younger son said, "I'm outta here," and hit-the-road traveling to a distant country. He lived the high life, squandering all his money on sex, drugs, and rock and roll. (OK, maybe not drugs and rock and roll, but you get the picture.) Luke tells us, "There was a severe famine in that whole country, and he began to be in need. So he went and hired himself out to a citizen of that country, who sent him to his fields to feed pigs. He longed to fill his stomach with the pods that the pigs were eating, but no one gave him anything" (Luke 15:14–16, NIV).

Finally, he came to his senses (I guess living with pigs gets old, real fast) and said, "*This is absurd, my father's hired men have food to spare and here I sit in the pigpen, starving.*" He decided to go back to his father and tell him, "Father, I have sinned against heaven and

> Throughout the Bible, the word *compassion* provides deep insight into God's compassionate heart.

against you. I am no longer worthy to be called your son; make me like one of your hired men" (Luke 15:18–19, NIV). The young man arose and started the journey back to his father. I just love this next verse: "But while he was still a long way off, his father saw him and was filled with compassion for him; he ran to his son, threw his arms around him and kissed him" (Luke 15:20, NIV).

Can you just picture the heartbroken father standing silently, looking down the road each day, hoping to see his son? Suddenly, his dream becomes reality. He sees him in the distance but doesn't wait for his son to arrive. He runs to meet him with outstretched arms and kisses him, crying tears of joy.

His son, repentant and broken, speaks to his father: "I have sinned against heaven and against you. I am no longer worthy to be called your son" (Luke 15:21, NIV). The father is so ecstatic that he doesn't reply directly to his son but, instead, tells his servants, "Quick! Bring the best robe and put it on him. Put a ring on his finger and sandals on his feet. Bring the fattened calf and kill it. Let's have a feast and celebrate. For this son of mine was dead and is alive again; he was lost and is found" (Luke 15:22–24, NIV).

As far as the father was concerned, he forgave his son; his loving response was enough to prove that. The father's heart of compassion made him expectantly wait for him to return; through compassion, he forgave his son—completely. So we can easily see by this parable that compassion and forgiveness go hand-in-hand (we'll look at forgiveness in greater depth in chapter 8).

Do you notice he didn't say, "See, I told you that you'd mess-up your life and come crawling back, begging for forgiveness?" Compassion only sees the person's wretched condition and wants to remove the suffering through any means possible. It doesn't consider how the person came to be in that state. Neither does it point fingers of accusation, nor say, "Well, it's your own fault you're in this mess," especially when it involves suffering as a result of bad choices or sin.

This timeless parable reflects how God reacts when we are apart from Him, living in sin. He waits patiently, longing for us to come back to Him for restoration. When we start our return on the road of repentance, He comes quickly to receive us with joy and forgive us. Psalm 103:13 describes God's compassion using a familiar example: "As a father has compassion on his children, so the LORD has compassion on those who fear him" (NIV). The following account from the book of Mark lets us see Jesus' heart of compassion in action.

Jesus had just performed miracles of healing on the western (Jewish) side of the Sea of Galilee. Shortly thereafter, He boarded a ship with His disciples and traveled to the eastern (Gentile) side of the sea. "During those days another large crowd gathered. Since they had nothing to eat, Jesus called his disciples to him and said, 'I have compassion for these people; they have already been with me three days and have nothing to eat. If I send them home hungry, they will collapse on the way, because some of them have come a long distance'" (Mark 8:1–3, NIV). Though His disciples had previously seen Jesus perform a similar miracle where He fed five thousand, His disciples answered, "'But where in this remote place can anyone get enough bread to feed them?' 'How many loaves do you have?' Jesus asked. 'Seven,' they replied. He told the crowd to sit down on the ground. When he had taken the seven loaves and given thanks, he broke them and gave them to his disciples to set before the people, and they did so. They had a few small fish as well; he gave thanks for them also and told the disciples to distribute them. The people ate and were satisfied. Afterward the disciples picked up seven basketfuls of broken pieces that were left over. About four thousand men were present" (Mark 8:1–9, NIV). If you search elsewhere in the Gospels, you will see that Jesus first experienced compassion, then did something to meet people's needs.

A COMPASSIONATE FOCUS

You may ask, "You have shown great examples of compassion, but what does this mean to me? I'm just an ordinary person." Good question, but first I must place everything in the proper perspective. The underlying theme of this book is that all it takes to show Big-Heartedness is to do what you can with what you have. It's about ordinary people doing extraordinary things.

God never asked Jesus to perform something He could not do. Similarly, God will never ask us to do anything that we do not have a gift for, or where He will not provide the means or ability to do it. We must remember that, "Where God guides, He provides." He may never ask you to feed a multitude with only a handful of provisions. However, He may ask you to cook a dinner and bring it to someone who is ill or disabled. God may never ask you to still the forces of nature with your command, but He may inspire you to speak comforting words to a hurting soul. Focus on what you *can do* instead of what you *can't do*, and step out in faith.

How does God carry out His perfect plan through you? He opens your eyes to see those who are suffering and fills your heart with compassion toward them. The words of Dietrich Bonhoeffer, German pastor and martyr, affirms this with deep conviction: "We must learn to regard people less in the light of what they do or omit to do, and more in the light of what they suffer."[8]

How often we have heard this spoken: "People do not care how much you know, until they know how much you care." Despite the popularity of this quote, the world at-large either doesn't understand it, or ignores it all together. To them, the worship of knowledge and intellect is preferable. They just haven't realized that those who care for their fellow human beings reveal an even higher knowledge—one based on a personal experience of knowing God's compassionate heart. Those who show compassion the most are those who received the most compassion. That is why each of us who experienced God's compassion and forgiveness through Jesus Christ should overflow with the same toward others.

Opening our hearts with compassion carries a certain vulnerability, which affirms the sincerity of our caring. Compassion moves us to reach out with genuine concern and care for people in need—making a difference. The Apostle Jude offers this scriptural confirmation:

> Keep yourselves in the love of God, looking for the mercy of our Lord Jesus Christ unto eternal life. And of some have compassion, making a difference.
>
> —JUDE 1:21–22, KJV

BIG-HEARTED TO A FAULT

Do you have a friend or family member who constantly helps others, even to the degree of emotional or physical exhaustion? Do you know a selfless person whom people always turn to when they have pressing needs? Usually, we use the phrase "Big-Hearted to a fault" to describe them. Possibly, you're one of these Big-Hearted People who can't stand to see others in great distress. You feel a personal obligation to help people, regardless of their needs or situation in life. However, when we reach out with compassion as Big-Hearted People, we should be mindful not to allow our emotions to dictate our response. We must rely on the Holy Spirit, through prayer, to give us wisdom about how best to meet the needs of those we wish to help. Of course, our first goal should always be to relieve their suffering if possible. And so, this is why I have highlighted different ways that we can respond to others, to help us avoid becoming Big-Hearted to a fault.

> Those who show compassion the most are those who received the most compassion.

Maybe your thinking goes something like this, "Jesus called us to reach out to the impoverished, hurting, or grief-stricken. I *must* respond to hurting people if I'm to be truly Christlike." You are certainly correct, because that's exactly what Jesus asks us to do. If your life demonstrates this, let me first compliment you for your Big Heart of compassion. The world needs more people like you.

Yet, if you develop health problems from overextending yourself, what value are you to others? Jesus realized His need to get away from people occasionally—to pray, rest, and rejuvenate. Jesus even stressed its importance to His disciples: "Then, because so many people were coming and going that they did not even have a chance to eat, he said to them, 'Come with me by yourselves to a quiet place and get some rest'" (Mark 6:31, NIV). Certainly, we could all benefit from heeding His words of wisdom.

Sometimes you find yourself caught in a cycle where you're helping the same people who always encounter the same problems. You help them, but it seems the more you do for them, the more they expect from you. If this happens frequently, you can do them more harm than good. By becoming an enabler, you create an unwholesome dependency where they identify you as their primary source of help. That's why it is important to teach them what God's Word says about learning how to trust the Lord themselves. It may also be necessary to provide them with Bible-based guidance in *practical* matters, to avoid falling back into similar crises. Often, it's appropriate to recommend assistance programs through faith-based or nonprofit organizations. This may be the best way to help those who need more support than you can provide.

Just because you're a Big-Hearted Person, it doesn't mean you always give people everything they want or even need. There may be times when you should back away altogether, entrust them into God's hands, and pray. He knows what's best for them, and He will take the responsibility to work in their lives to bring about good. It isn't easy, but at times, it's necessary.

THE FAR REACH OF COMPASSION

The far-reaching results from a single act of compassion may not be evident immediately. Yet with the passage of time, it can yield great benefits exponentially. As we look into the ancient history of God's people in Egypt, we see a king rise to power who did not know Joseph or his covenant with God.

He puts his thumb down on the Hebrew people and afflicts them as slaves to build his treasure cities. Despite their treatment, the Hebrew people grow in numbers until Pharaoh fears they will eventually overtake Egypt. In response, He issues an edict to cast every son born to Hebrew households into the river and only save the daughters.

Jochebed, a woman from the house of Levi, bears a son, and in compassion, she spares his life by hiding him for three months. In her heart of hearts, she knows that God's hand is on her son and that he *must* live. When it's no longer safe to hide him at home, she devises a plan to keep him alive. She lays him in a basket and places it in the river, telling his older sister to watch where it floats.

What she sees next unfolds as an account in the book of Exodus: "Then the daughter of Pharaoh came down to bathe at the river. And her maidens walked along the riverside; and when she saw the ark among the reeds, she sent her maid to get it. And when she opened it, she saw the child, and behold, the baby wept. So she had *compassion* on him, and said, 'This is one of the Hebrews' children'" (Exod. 2:5–6, NKJV, author's emphasis).

Pharaoh's daughter reacts unexpectedly, since the Egyptians consider the Hebrews as no more than chattel. I believe the Lord gives her a heart of compassion to bring about His great plan to save Israel. The baby's sister draws near to Pharaoh's daughter and asks, "Shall I find a Hebrew woman to nurse the child for you?" She responds, "Go," and the girl went straight to her mother who then becomes the nursemaid to her own son. Pharaoh's daughter adopts him as her own and names him Moses. I'm sure you already know the rest of the story. Moses becomes God's instrument to deliver His people from bondage in Egypt, and God brings them into the Promised Land.

Single acts of compassion by two women, Jochebed and Pharaoh's daughter, coincide to become the means through which millions of Hebrews escape the cruel slavery of Egypt. Taking this even further, Moses as the Hebrews' deliverer foreshadows the ultimate deliverance of mankind by Jesus Christ.

We have no idea how far one Big-Hearted act of compassion might reach. Let us realize that the compassion we show may eventually bring about good in the lives of multitudes, not only in this life but also for eternity.

4

SELF-SACRIFICE

Self-preservation is the first law of nature; self-sacrifice the highest rule of grace.

—Anonymous[1]

During the last half-century, we have seen dramatic attempts to exclude religion from our modern culture. It didn't happen overnight, but occurred slowly and with great resolve. We are also experiencing an increase of indifference to the well-being of others. In addition, current trends show an intense focus on the personal expression of "self" in one form or another. For example, we often hear about the concepts of self-esteem, self-awareness, self-realization, and self-improvement. Some of these methods simply began as ways to attain desirable qualities; but eventually, they morphed into inner-focused elements comprising the "cult of self." Richard Cecil, an Anglican minister of another century, spoke of the self-nature in this way: "The very heart and root of sin is an independent spirit. We erect the idol self, and not only wish others to worship it but worship it ourselves."[2]

One can easily find plenty of products, Web sites, and publications that cater to feeling good about or improving one's self. So it's no surprise the term *self-sacrifice* seems increasingly alien. Why is the notion of sacrificing for others altogether rejected by some people, or in the least, relegated to the "too hard" category? What comprises self-sacrifice? How does it apply to being a Big-Hearted Person? In this chapter, I will answer these questions and show how we can trust God to help us make this attribute a personal reality.

GIVE UP AND TAKE UP

God is a God of order and balance; the Scripture states that He "changes not." However, like a pendulum, humanity precariously swings from one extreme to another. In his work *The City of God,* St. Augustine highlights two: "The world has been controlled by two parties: those who have governed by *"love of self to the point of contempt of God"* and those who have governed by *"love of God to the point of contempt of self."*[3] Here he implies that both extremes are the "way of the world."

As Christians, the Bible cautions us not to adapt to the world and its ways. So in response, we see that it is necessary to change our thinking patterns to line up with the Word of God: "And do not be conformed to this world, but be transformed by the renewing of your mind, that you may prove what is that good and acceptable and perfect will of God" (Rom. 12:2, NKJV). As we consider these words, let's look at self-sacrifice in a balanced approach and as defined within the pages of Scripture.

When one closely examines the diverse ways to use the word *sacrifice,* a central theme presents itself with perfect clarity. Whether used in a sacred or secular context, the underlying principles are still the same. First, there must always be an offering or the loss of something considered valuable or precious. Second, the sacrifice made is for the sake of obtaining something more valuable or for greater gain. Equally, a sacrifice may be for the benefit of someone considered to be of great worth or someone deserving homage or worship. You could also define self-sacrifice as the willingness to set aside one's own self-interests or agenda in exchange for certain ideals, or for people whose needs are more urgent than our own.

A man came home after the last war with an empty coat sleeve. A tactless neighbor said, "I see you've lost your arm." The veteran answered sharply, "I didn't lose it. I gave it."[4] This brief account embodies a great example of self-sacrifice. There are many who gave their physical well-being and lives for their country to keep the dreams of hope and freedom alive. Jesus shared what He considered to be the greatest sacrifice—giving up one's life: "No one has greater love [no one has shown stronger affection] than to lay down (give up) his own life for his friends" (John 15:13, AMP).

However, most of us will never make such dramatic and all-consuming sacrifices; but rather, smaller ones regularly. Self-sacrifice in its simplest form begins with changing our thought patterns to not always needing to have everything go our way, or preferring others above ourselves.

I believe there is a practical way that Big-Hearted People can demonstrate self-sacrifice in the day-to-day activities of life. When we read what Jesus said about it, we discover that He asks us to do two things: give up and take up.

- Give up (spend) our lives for others.
- Take up our cross and follow Him.

Jesus called the people and His followers to Him. He said to them, "If anyone wants to be My follower, he must give up himself and his own desires. He must take up his cross and follow Me. If anyone wants to keep his own life safe, he will lose it. If anyone gives up his life because of Me and because of the Good News, he will save it" (Mark 8:34–35, New Life). The King James Bible uses the word *deny* in place of *give up*. Jesus was saying directly, "Deny your*self*"; there is no mistaking His intent. This suggests activity, not passivity. The world says the opposite: "Please your*self*," "Look out for number one," or "I can have it all."

Many people avoid self-sacrifice or reject it all together. Why? Because it means they have to give up their wants, comfort, or ambitions for the sake of something or somebody. It may mean "going without" for a time, which is in direct conflict with our current "I want it now" society. Many hold on tightly to things considered dear and don't see the real blessing self-sacrifice can produce. They consider it difficult and costly, and they simply do not want to pay the price.

Yet, what does Jesus mean when He tells us to take up our cross? Is the cross He asks us to bear a burden of sickness, poverty, disaster, or death of a loved one? Absolutely not! Jesus was inferring that the cross is what occurs when we deny ourselves—when we go against everything our self-centered mind and heart are telling us, and live for others and for Him. That's what the cross represents.

In Jesus' day, the worst form of death was crucifixion. The Romans perfected it to the degree where it inflicted the worst possible pain and suffering on the victim. So when Jesus spoke about the cross to His disciples, they understood the seriousness of His statement. Yet, Jesus' death on the cross brought about the most wonderful blessing for mankind—salvation and eternal life. Without the cross, the human race would have been doomed to eternal death.

Let's face the facts; it isn't easy to set aside our own will, desires, and ambitions in preference for God, and especially for other people. It's painful to die to ourselves. But when we take up our cross, we'll begin to see that it's not some morbid, grin-and-bear-it duty; but something that produces a harvest of blessing in others and actually brings us great joy.

The pressure to conform to the world surrounds us daily. We need to decide whether to follow Jesus' truth or the world's lies. The choice is clear: give up your life for others and save it, or hold onto it tightly and lose it. The Message Bible further amplifies Jesus' words in the previous verse with modern language: "Calling the crowd to join his disciples, he said, 'Anyone who intends to come with me has to let me lead. You're not in the driver's seat; I am. Don't run from suffering; embrace it. Follow me and I'll show you how. Self-help is no help at all. Self-sacrifice is the way, my way, to saving yourself, your true self. What good would it do to get everything you want and lose you, the real you? What could you ever trade your soul for?'" (Mark 8:34–37, THE MESSAGE).

The word *life* comes from the Greek word *psuche* or the more familiar *psychē*, which refers to the soul. Jesus was telling His disciples and us to lay down our own feelings, desires, or affections for His sake and the sake of others. That is the truth of self-sacrifice and the essence of Big-Heartedness.

THE BOND OF SELF-SACRIFICE

Acts of self-sacrifice form a cultural adhesive that bond friends, families, communities, and, ultimately, society together. One reason the family unit is so fragile and sometimes broken is that some people naturally gravitate to *selfishness* and resist *self-sacrifice*. Mothers are aborting the precious lives of their unborn children. Fathers don't accept their paternal responsibilities and become deadbeat Dads. Divorces cause great harm to husbands, wives, and children alike. We live in a fractured society. Self-sacrifice should start in the home. If we aren't selfless to our own family members, how can we be selfless toward anyone else?

> Acts of self-sacrifice form a cultural adhesive that bond friends, families, communities, and, ultimately, society together.

Most parents are familiar with self-sacrifice and probably can identify with this example. Early in our married life before we had children, my wife and I made decisions that we knew required sacrifice, one of which would necessitate her staying at home with our children instead of pursuing a career. There were times when it wasn't easy and it cost us financially. Twelve years of marriage passed before we were able to buy our first house. Yet, we're glad we made those decisions because today we enjoy the blessings that resulted from doing what we felt God was asking us to do. Our children are now adults, serving the Lord, and they have given us seven wonderful grandchildren.

How does this apply to your church family? What part does self-sacrifice play toward other members of the body of Christ? John, the beloved apostle, describes it in this way:

> This is how we've come to understand and experience love: Christ sacrificed his life for us. This is why we ought to live sacrificially for our fellow believers, and not just be out for ourselves. If you see some brother or sister in need and have the means to do something about it but turn a cold shoulder and do nothing, what happens to God's love? It disappears. And you made it disappear.
>
> —1 John 3:16–17, The Message

The Life of Self-sacrifice

Who are those making a difference in the lives of individuals, families, and nations? Big-Hearted People! They are not strangers to sacrifice and have learned to count the cost. They conclude the sacrifices they make, no matter how small, will produce great benefits in the lives of others.

Big-Hearted People are willing to sacrifice their own dreams so others can achieve theirs. They follow the One who made the greatest sacrifice for them, Jesus Christ. Take a moment now and think about the sacrifice God made to purchase our salvation. It cost Him everything—the dearest, most costly sacrifice He could make—the life of His only Son, Jesus. He could give nothing greater and sacrificed His all for you and me—sinful, wretched mankind. "But God put his love on the line for us by offering his Son in sacrificial death while we were of no use whatever to him" (Romans 5:8, The Message). When we think about Jesus' consummate sacrifice, is any sacrifice we make for Him or fellow human beings too great?

Some people seem naturally selfless. Though they realize there is a cost associated with self-sacrifice, they are more willing to give up personal dreams, pleasures, and comforts to bless others. In contrast, there are people who wish to become more selfless but struggle because they haven't given an ultimatum to their self-life. They find it hard to die to their own self-desires. Possibly, some of us are in this latter category.

> Big-Hearted People are willing to sacrifice their own dreams so others can achieve theirs.

How can self-sacrifice increasingly become a part of our everyday walk with Jesus? If we use our own strength and determination, it becomes our own work and we will surely fail. A "What's in it for me?" lifestyle doesn't become a "What's in it for others?" mindset overnight. Nineteenth-century minister

Frederick William Robertson explained the fallacy of sacrifice without the Spirit of God: "Sacrifice alone, bare and unrelieved, is ghastly, unnatural, and dead; but self-sacrifice, illuminated by love, is warmth, and life; it is the death of Christ, the life of God, and the blessedness and only proper life of man."[5]

To experience this Big-Hearted attribute, you must take the first step. Ask God in faith, and believe the Holy Spirit will place opportunities before you to show self-sacrifice to others. Then make the choice to rely on Him, and as you do, He will enable you, by His grace, to demonstrate self-sacrifice as a Big-Hearted Person.

5

SELFLESS GIVING

You can give without loving, but you cannot love without giving.

—Amy Carmichael[1]

This particular Saturday morning was far less humid than just a few days before. The temperature had started its decline and was more typical of the usual weather in Florida during autumn. I decided to spend time with my youngest daughter and make a trip to the downtown public library to borrow some books and videos. I parked the car alongside beautiful Lake Eola and enjoyed watching the regal swans serenely float along the water's edge. The lake's fountain filled the air with mist, and the tiny droplets seemed to dance as they reflected the morning sun. Walking together on the sidewalk, we noticed a homeless person, one of many who visited the area. Expectedly disheveled, his lack of proper nutrition was obvious by his thin appearance. On further observation, I watched as he left the park area and headed toward us on the same sidewalk.

The human mind, not surprisingly, begins to play invented scenarios of what could possibly transpire in the coming moments. Would he merely walk by without speaking a word, or throw a glance in our direction? Could he be one of those "crazed" homeless people who would point his boney finger at us and scream obscenities? Would he stop and ask for some help; and if so, what would be our response? I tried not to show a hint of anything unusual in front of my daughter.

Just a few seconds later, we came within speaking distance. Though I did my best not to acknowledge his impending presence, my eye caught his, and he probably sensed something that made him stop. He faced me as if it were only he and I standing there. His expression revealed a deeply wounded life as he briefly spoke, "You got some lose change? I haven't eaten nuthin' today." The smell of alcohol accompanied each slowly spoken word. Immediately, I thought I knew the *real* reason he wanted the money.

I quickly answered with a typical response that often precedes those caught in an uncomfortable moment, "I'm sorry; not today." He lowered his head and kept walking as if my response didn't surprise him. To justify my obvious indifference, I commented to my daughter, "He's just a beggar trying to get money so he can buy alcohol to feed his addiction." Without a moment's pause, God spoke to my spirit and said, "Why should it matter to you what he will use the money for? You missed an opportunity to show your daughter how wonderful it is to give to someone in need."

Now, please realize that I'm not recommending that we give to everyone always, without even thinking. If we did, we'd be acting in presumption instead of faith. Rather, we should take suitable opportunities to show God's love through giving as the Holy Spirit leads us. Though I wish I could, there was no way to go back and relive that moment. However, I received an important lesson that made a significant impact in my life. Since that event, I have always taught my children and grandchildren by word and deed that, as Jesus once said, "It is more blessed to give than receive."

THE DEPTH OF SELFLESS GIVING

Throughout the fabric of the Bible, we clearly see the weave of a common theme. God is a giver. He cannot do otherwise; it is His consummate nature. In truth, God gave all He could give to redeem the human race and give us eternal life. John 3:16–17 tells us, "*For God so loved* the world *that He gave* His only begotten Son, that whoever believes in Him should not perish but have everlasting life. For God did not send His Son into the world to condemn the world, but that the world through Him might be saved" (NKJV, emphasis added). From Genesis to Revelation, we see how God continually interacts with mankind with a heart of giving. So since selfless giving is an integral part of His character, how does He expect us to demonstrate the same spirit of giving as His Big-Hearted People?

To illustrate the simplicity and depth of selfless giving, I will recount two stories from the Gospels. Both examples seem a bit extreme and not what you would normally think of when pondering this attribute. Yet, they can provide us with wisdom to be more effective in giving selflessly—as Big-Hearted People.

No doubt, many of us have read about the poor widow whom Jesus used as an example of selfless giving. Let us revisit the narrative as described in the twelfth chapter of Mark's Gospel:

> Jesus sat down opposite the place where the offerings were put and watched the crowd putting their money into the temple treasury. Many rich people threw in large amounts. But a poor widow came and put in two very small copper coins, worth only a fraction of a penny. Calling his disciples to him, Jesus said, "I tell you the truth, this poor widow has put more into the treasury than all the others. They all gave out of their wealth; but she, out of her poverty, put in everything—all she had to live on."
>
> —MARK 12:41–44, NIV

This poor woman's sacrificial offering describes selfless giving perfectly. In great need herself, she trusted God with complete and total abandon. She knew He would faithfully take care of her needs regardless of the circumstances.

Another biblical account describes an ordinary woman named Mary. She freely gave herself to reckless living and the depths of sin. As a result, she experienced the scorn of the pompous religious leaders. Her reputation with the townsfolk was broken beyond repair. Mary, the party animal, decided to become the party crasher—but didn't care; she was desperate. She only had one chance and would give it her best shot, no matter the cost. There was simply no one else to turn to except Jesus, the lowly Nazarene.

> God is a giver. He cannot do otherwise; it is His consummate nature.

The following account comes from the Gospels of Luke and Matthew. (See Luke 7:37–50; Matthew 26:6–13, KJV.) Broken and humble, she approached the only one who could understand the secrets of her heart.

> As Jesus sat at dinner in Simon (the Pharisee's) house, she brought an alabaster box of costly ointment, and poured it on his head. She stood at his feet behind him weeping, and began to wash his feet with tears, wiped them with the hairs of her head, kissed his feet, and anointed them with the ointment. But when his disciples saw it, they were indignant, saying, to what purpose is this waste? For this ointment might have been sold, and given to the poor. When Jesus heard it he said, Why do you trouble the woman? She has wrought a good work upon me. You have the poor always with you but you

do not have me with you always. She has poured this ointment on my body for my burial. *Most of those in the room had no idea what He was talking about.* "Truly I say unto you, wherever this good news shall be preached in the whole world, this shall also be told for a memorial of her. Her sins, which are many, are forgiven; for she loved much, but to whom little is forgiven, the same loves little. And he said unto her, your sins are forgiven, your faith has saved you; go in peace."

It was a selfless act from a woman viewed by others as a person of no account. It's possible she spent all her money to buy this ointment. She poured it on Jesus, not realizing she was actually anointing Him for his burial. With a contrite heart, she gave Him what she could give. He told her that He forgave her sins, and like a parched soul in need of water, she quenched her thirst from the well of His forgiveness. Over the centuries, Mary's memory has received honor because of her extraordinary act of selfless giving.

None of us will ever give selflessly to the person of Jesus Christ in such a dramatic way as did Mary. However, when we show love and kindness through giving, Jesus considers it the same as if we did it to Him. He said, "Assuredly, I say to you, inasmuch as you did it to one of the least of these My brethren, you did it to Me" (Matt. 25:40, NKJV).

With the previous examples in mind, I certainly don't support giving away everything we own to become poor and destitute ourselves. Though, I would be amiss if I didn't highlight biblical accounts about giving that God viewed as important enough to include in the Gospels. Remember, God is always in a giving mode. He gives to us so we in turn can give to others. So how can we be more faithful in our giving? This begins when we prayerfully change our minds from looking inward to please ourselves to looking outward to bless people. When we do, we will start to see new opportunities to give selflessly.

WISE INVESTING—HEAVENLY DIVIDENDS

I've heard it said that you can tell a person's priorities by looking at his or her checkbook. I'm in total agreement. Personal credits and debits can reveal much about the true nature of someone's heart as it relates to giving. Some people in the world today give little and save little, if at all. They accumulate enormous debt and live paycheck to paycheck. Sometimes, this forces families to rely on two paychecks, and if either spouse loses their job, they're in serious financial trouble. This is not God's best for us.

Maybe you're someone who doesn't give a percentage of your finances regularly, but you would like to; or maybe you give, but it's less than you want. An easy way to start is to use the 10–10–80 method. Put God first by giving 10 percent to His work (in blessing others). Then save 10 percent, and live on the remaining 80 percent. This may require some sacrifice at first. But if you're faithful, you will begin to experience God's prosperity and the peace that comes with it. Then stretch your faith to give more, and you will see the law of reciprocity (give and it will be given to you) begin to take effect.

If you're already a Big-Hearted giver, these words of scripture probably affirm what you already know:

> He who has pity on the poor lends to the Lord, and that which he has given He will repay to him.
> —PROVERBS 19:17, AMP

> Let everyone give but not reluctantly or because they feel compelled to give, for God takes pleasure in people who delight in giving. Remember that those who sow sparingly will also reap sparingly, and those who sow generously will also reap generously.
> —2 CORINTHIANS 9:6–7, AUTHOR'S PARAPHRASE

If God has given us abilities that enable us to prosper financially, it's not so we can live the self-centered "good life." Now, I don't mean to infer that we shouldn't enjoy our lives. I wholeheartedly believe that God wants us to experience an abundant life in all its fullness but not to exclude others. A life lived for oneself is unsatisfying, empty, and sad. Jesus encouraged us to give by saying, "Freely you have received, freely give" (Matt. 10:8, NIV)

I once had a conversation with a multimillionaire who shared some personal reasons for his success. He stressed the importance of giving by telling me that he donates over fifty percent of his income to bless others. He didn't share this for me to regard him as someone special but to recognize that he serves a faithful God who wants to bless people. Can money buy happiness? It certainly can—if we spend it to make others happy! Generous giving also has physiological benefits for the giver, too. The good feeling you get when you give from a full heart comes because giving stimulates the release of dopamine, a feel-good hormone that calms your brain. Let us learn to give with a strong faith that says, "Whatever God asks me to give, I'll give it heartily and joyfully because I know He is faithful to meet my needs."

I strongly believe that when we give in faith, we receive it back to us multiplied. The Scriptures overwhelmingly confirm this:

> Give, and it will be given to you. A good measure, pressed down, shaken together and running over, will be poured into your lap. For with the measure you use, it will be measured to you.
>
> —LUKE 6:38, NIV

> Honor the Lord with your capital and sufficiency [from righteous labors] and with the firstfruits of all your income; So shall your storage places be filled with plenty, and your vats shall be overflowing with new wine.
>
> —PROVERBS 3:9–10, AMP

And remember, the Lord can also give back to us in ways other than just financial provision. I'm especially fond of this verse about giving; it's so simple, yet it reveals a great truth: "The man who gives much will have much, and he who helps others will be helped himself" (Prov. 11:25, NEW LIFE).

If God has given us abilities that enable us to prosper financially, it's not so we can live the self-centered "good life."

My wife and I have two dear Big-Hearted friends, Doug and Mary, who are now in their eighties. We have known them for over thirty-five years, and they are kind and generous people. Their income consists of two small pensions and Social Security. When they retired more than twenty years ago, they made a commitment that goes against popular retirement strategies. They pledged to give her entire pension (the larger one) to the Lord's work. Since then, they have never lacked for anything. By exercising their faith, God has prospered them and given them the added benefits of joy and peace.

Why are they so generous in their giving? Did they wake up one morning and suddenly decide to become Big-Hearted givers? The answer is twofold. They learned the principle of selfless giving through God's Word and by the example of others.

During the Great Depression, Doug's parents often responded to knocks on the door by needy people. Mostly, they were asking if there were odd jobs they could do in exchange for pay or food. Though there was no need for handiwork around the home, they never turned anyone away empty handed. Either they treated the needy to a warm meal or gave them clothing or money. Doug's parents were faithful in sharing their provision with others. God responded by providing them with enough for themselves and some left over to give out.

Big-Hearted People are always looking for opportunities to give—at home, in their communities, and worldwide. Some of us may not have the means to travel the globe to help people, but we can still make a difference in people's lives everywhere. You can easily find many domestic and worldwide outreaches that offer aid to those you might not be able to help directly. My wife and I give to worldwide ministries, and through them, we can see Big-Hearted benevolence touching people's lives everywhere by:

- Drilling wells to provide fresh water to third world countries.
- Providing on-site medical and dental services to people who do not have health care clinics available.
- Setting up vocational training and micro-enterprise development.
- Offering health and sanitation education programs.
- Providing meals, personal hygiene items, and construction help to victims of natural disasters.
- Offering adoptions, academic and life-skills training, and health programs for orphans.

Maybe you give to similar organizations, and if so, only eternity will reveal how many lives you touched through your generosity. There are honest and trustworthy charities the world over that have pure motives and genuine dedication to bless others. However, make sure you perform thorough research before you give. Sadly, some charities advertise that your money is helping people, but only a small percentage reaches those who need it most. There are other organizations that are just plain predatory. This is another reason Jesus warned us to be "wise as serpents but as harmless as doves" (Matt. 10:16, KJV).

Selfless Receivers

Big-Hearted People are givers and find it easy and comfortable. Most act immediately if someone asks them for a favor but are reluctant to ask for one themselves. They give so often that they sometimes find it difficult to receive. Selfless givers also need to learn how to be selfless receivers. It's an act of Big-Heartedness to allow someone to give to us. Sometimes we don't realize that our willingness to receive can become a source of blessing to somebody else.

Whenever anyone gives, a double blessing occurs—one for the recipient and one for the giver. When we find ourselves on the receiving end we often think of saying, "Thanks, but you really shouldn't have done this," especially when the giver is someone of less means than ourselves. Some people might even want to repay the giver in some way. This may sound harsh, but if we don't accept their generosity, we are robbing them of the blessing that normally follows an act of giving. Just receive the gift graciously and thank the giver for their kindness.

A great way to do this is to send a personal thank you card with a hand-written message (not an e-mail). It shows them that you took time to select a card and write heartfelt words of gratitude. Personal cards and letters written by hand are rapidly becoming a relic of the past. This makes them even more special and appreciated.

Can money buy happiness? It certainly can—if we spend it to make others happy!

With these thoughts in mind, let's look at receiving as it applies to our relationship with God. Due to our fallen nature, we may find it hard to receive from God. We sometimes have the mistaken impression that we should do something to merit His gifts. Maybe we think it's necessary to make a personal sacrifice or do a selfless act for someone in order to please God. In truth, we please Him just as we are—in Christ. Since God delights in giving, He wants us to receive from Him with joy and thanksgiving. Remember the words of Jesus: "Ask and receive that your joy may be full" (John 16:24). Jesus did not qualify this statement by telling us what we should or shouldn't ask for. He gave us a blank check. Some may take exception by saying, "This only promotes greed; besides, it makes God out to be nothing more than a heavenly Santa Claus."

Well, then, let's see what the Scriptures reveal about God's willingness to give to us.

> If even evil people know how to give good gifts to their children, how much more will God your Father give good gifts to you if you simply ask Him.
>
> —MATTHEW 7:11, AUTHOR'S PARAPHRASE

> The Lord gives favor and honor. He holds back nothing good from those who walk in the way that is right. Lord of all, how happy is the man who trusts in You!
>
> —PSALM 84:11, NEW LIFE

If our hearts are in tune with God by agreeing with His Word, I don't believe we will ask just to indulge our own sensual pleasures. Let us always remember that as Big-Hearted People, God wants us to experience fullness of joy as both givers *and* receivers.

ANONYMOUSLY YOURS

Occasionally our deeds of kindness and giving receive public notice or the one who receives knows our identity. Sometimes this is hard to avoid. It's possible that this will even be necessary to give us an opportunity to share God's love and faithfulness with someone. When we give a gift, it's only natural for the recipient to want to thank us for it. However, the temptation to take pride in our generosity is ever present. We must be careful not to become "gratitude collectors." With this in mind, our goal should be to give where there is no clue about who performed the act of Big-Heartedness. In this way, the greater glory will go to God since He inspired us to do it in the first place.

> Whenever anyone gives, a double blessing occurs—one for the recipient and one for the giver.

Twelfth-century Jewish rabbi and scholar Moses Maimonides divided what he considered to be the Golden Rule into eight graduated levels of charity. The second-highest level is the *matan b'seter* or "giving in secret," which occurs when the giver does not know to whom they give, nor does the recipient know from whom he or she is receiving. This directly lines up with the teachings of Jesus, who stressed this during His Sermon on the Mount:

> Be especially careful when you are trying to be good so that you don't make a performance out of it. It might be good theater, but the God who made you won't be applauding. When you do something for someone else, don't call attention to yourself. You've seen them in action, I'm sure—"playactors" I call them—treating prayer meeting and street corner alike as a stage, acting compassionate as long as someone is watching, playing to the crowds. They get applause, true, but that's all they get. When you help someone out, don't think about how it looks. Just do it—quietly and unobtrusively. That is the way your God, who conceived you in love, working behind the scenes, helps you out.
>
> —MATTHEW 6:1–4, THE MESSAGE

Jesus was saying that if you give to draw attention to yourself, your motives are impure. God is not as concerned with how much we give but why we give.

GIFTS OF TIME

Normally money comes to mind when we think about giving, yet we can give in other ways as well. One is to give the gift of time by passing along knowledge or expertise through mentoring. About thirty-four years ago, I decided to learn calligraphy (the term comes from the Greek words *kallos* ["beauty"] and *graph* ["writing"] and literally means "beautiful writing"). As hard as I tried to learn on my own, it was clear that I needed a teacher. I knew that I must attend classes and workshops if I wanted to improve my calligraphy skills. Through a series of circumstances—which I won't recount for the sake of brevity—I met someone who made a marked difference in my life. His name was Walter Filling, a gentle, modest man who was a master engraver and calligrapher. For twenty-seven years, he operated a studio in the National Press Building in Washington, D.C. He often created calligraphy for the White House and United States Senate.

Walter and I developed a friendship in the mid 1970s. I expressed to him that I had an interest in learning the art of calligraphy and manuscript illumination. He agreed to teach me and serve as my mentor. Though he eventually retired to his family farm in Pennsylvania, we corresponded via phone and mail. On occasion, I visited him to get in-depth training. For almost twenty years, he taught me everything he knew and never charged me a dime. Eventually, my calligraphy skills improved so much that our mutual friends commented that they could not tell the difference between my work and his. Unfortunately, he passed away in 1997. Yet even then, his giving lived on because he made me the heir of his tools of the trade. From his wealth of knowledge, he gave a unique gift to a young man who was willing and eager to learn. This was Walter's special way of giving something of lasting value. His gift carries on through my hands, and by God's grace, I have used it to bless others.

Christian discipleship closely relates to mentoring but is accomplished, more specifically, within a biblical framework. A person who disciples is one who trains another (or others) to pattern their life according to the teachings of Jesus. In His own words, Jesus told us what it meant to be His disciple: "If you abide in My word [hold fast to My teachings and live in accordance with them], you are truly My disciples. And you will know the Truth, and the Truth will set you free" (John 8:31–32, AMP). He also gave us a mandate to make disciples throughout the world: "Therefore go and make disciples of all nations, baptizing them in the name of the Father and of the Son and of the Holy Spirit, and teaching them to obey everything I have commanded you. And surely I am with you always, to the very end of the age" (Matt. 28:19–20, NIV). Do you want to follow Jesus' teachings? Do you want to know how to abide in His Word and live for Him and for others? Then one sure way is to ask a mature Christian to disciple you. Or maybe you're someone who could disciple Christians who are young in the faith.

I can easily draw on a practicable example from my own life to highlight the importance of Christian discipling. My wife and I were young Christians and had been married about a year when Jasper and Helen, a husband and wife from our church (about the same age as our parents), approached us. They asked us—in addition to some other young couples from church—to take part in a weekly Bible study and prayer time. It was a great opportunity for Christian fellowship and learning, so we gladly agreed to attend. Those of us with young children brought them. Our gracious hosts provided small cribs and beds where the children slept as we studied and prayed. Many young people came and went over the years, but some of us consistently attended—week after week, year after year.

Through this close-knit discipleship training, we received a solid foundation with which we lived our Christian faith. The added blessing was receiving wisdom and knowledge to raise our children in God's nurture and admonition. I can say without hesitation that this was the most important training my wife

> God is not as concerned with how much we give but why we give.

and I ever received. We passed these biblical principles on to our children. Now they also are doing the same with their families. Three generations received positive influence by the truth and precepts of God's Word—all because of two faithful, Big-Hearted People's selfless giving.

Are you sowing the truth of God's Word into the lives of people? Are you making a gift of your time to bless someone? Do you have certain abilities or mastered skills that you could pass on to others? If you are a Big-Hearted Person, then I am sure you can answer with a resounding *yes!*

Allow me to share verses from an anonymous poet that concisely describe the heart and soul of selfless giving.

> Give strength, give thought, give deeds, give wealth;
> Give love, give tears, and give thyself.
> Give, give, be always giving.
> Who gives not is not living;
> The more you give, the more you live.[2]

6

UNCONDITIONAL LOVE

Love seeketh not itself to please,
Nor for itself hath any care,
But for another gives its ease,
And builds a Heaven in Hell's despair.[1]

—WILLIAM BLAKE (1757–1827)

THE LANGUAGE OF LOVE

The English language has only one word to describe love. This is unfortunate, because the word *love* then becomes all-inclusive unless its use reveals the intended meaning. In contrast, there are four Greek words that describe different types of love, and each have their own distinct characteristics. A brief look at these words will help us better understand the Big-Hearted attribute of unconditional love.

The Greek word for God's perfect love is *agapē*. It is the same word for love we find described in one of the Pauline epistles: "But God had so much loving-kindness. He loved us with such a great love. Even when we were dead because of our sins, He made us alive by what Christ did for us. We have been saved from the punishment of sin by His loving-favor. God raised us up from death when He raised up Christ Jesus. He has given us a place with Christ in the heavens" (Eph. 2:4–6, NEW LIFE). God loves because He is love. His love is complete, selfless, all-encompassing, and without condition. We cannot earn His love based on what we do or don't do. God loves us just as we are—His highest creation. The Scriptures declare that Christ's love surpasses knowledge. Have you ever tried to share this with someone who has never heard about the love of Jesus Christ? Sometimes it's just too much for them to understand. Think about how strange it sounds to some people:

God Almighty comes to Earth and lives among humanity—His crea-
tion. He experiences great sorrow, grief, suffering and rejection by His
own people. Yet He shows His unconditional love by allowing humans
to execute Him by crucifixion—as He bears the sins of mankind. He
rises from the dead and offers forgiveness of sins and eternal life to
those who believe in Him.

That's enough to make an intellectual's head spin! To the world this is
nothing but foolishness, a cunningly devised fable. The Bible takes aim at this
and hits the target: "But God has chosen what the world calls foolish to shame
the wise. He has chosen what the world calls weak to shame what is strong.
God has chosen what is weak and foolish of
the world, what is hated and not known, to
destroy the things the world trusts in" (1 Cor.
1:27–28, New Life). It also tells us that "The
man without the Spirit does not accept the
things that come from the Spirit of God, for
they are foolishness to him, and he cannot
understand them, because they are spiritually discerned" (1 Cor. 2:14, NIV).

> We cannot earn His love
> based on what we do or don't
> do. God loves us just as we
> are—His highest creation.

God's love is so incredible that it actually takes His grace for us to believe
it's as true and wonderful as it sounds. He chooses to reveal it to those with
simple, childlike faith. Once we experience the love of Christ that passes understanding, He assures us that nothing will ever separate us from His love. (See
Romans 8:38–39.)

As we study God's Word we discover a threefold expression of His love
through Christ.

He *shows* His love *to* us:

> God has shown His love to us by sending His only Son into the
> world. God did this so we might have life through Christ.
> —1 John 4:9, New Life

He *places* His love *in* us:

> And hope does not disappoint us, because God has poured out his
> love into our hearts by the Holy Spirit, whom he has given us.
> —Romans 5:5, NIV

He demonstrates His love through us:

And may the Master pour on the love so it fills your lives and splashes over on everyone around you, just as it does from us to you.

—1 THESSALONIANS 3:12, THE MESSAGE

The second Greek word for love, *phileō*, describes a loyal, friendly, or brotherly love. The same root word appears in the name Philadelphia, referred to as the "city of brotherly love." Paul refers to this love in his letter to Titus when he writes, "Everyone with me sends you greetings. Greet those who love us in the faith. Grace be with you all" (Titus 3:15, NIV).

Third is the Greek word *storgē*, which defines the love characteristic of natural affection but is used only to show love relationships within the family, for example, the love parents show for their children.

The three previous types of love are not necessarily exclusive in themselves but can overlap one another depending on their usage.

The fourth word for love in Greek is *érōs*, from which comes the word *erotic*. Often found in both classical and modern literature, it describes a passionate, sensual, or sexual love. However, to stay within the subject matter of this chapter, I will not address this fourth love.

Neural scientists have proven there is a section of our brain that craves love from the time of our birth until the time we die. It's known as the limbic system. Since God created us with an internal yearning for love, this comes as no surprise. Emotional wounds occur when this inner need goes unfulfilled. Depending on their severity, these wounds can take a lifetime to heal. Often various addictions and physiological disorders result if they are not addressed, and they become ineffective substitutes for the love never received. If the English proverb "Love makes the world go round" is true, then the opposite is true as well—"Without love, the world plunges into chaos." Daily news reports confirm this with plenty of evidence.

THAT YOUR JOY MAY BE FULL

Shortly before His death, Jesus shared intimate communion with His disciples by opening His heart to them. He knew they'd soon experience heartache and grief and wanted to give them His comfort and peace. Let's take a moment to view this through a personal example so we can grasp the event's significance.

Suppose, for whatever reason, you only had a few days to live; what would you tell your family and friends? I'm sure you'd dig deep into your heart to share your love and the most important things you wanted them to remember forever—I would. And so it was with Jesus as He spoke these words to His disciples:

> Little children, I will be with you only a little while...I give you a new Law. You are to love each other. You must love each other as I have loved you. If you love each other, all men will know you are My followers. Later, He stressed it again to ensure they fully understood the depth of love He expected them to show and the reward if they obeyed: "I have loved you just as My Father has loved Me. Stay in My love. If you obey My teaching, you will live in My love. In this way, I have obeyed My Father's teaching and live in His love. I have told you these things so My joy may be in you and your joy may be full. This is what I tell you to do: Love each other just as I have loved you."
>
> —John 13:33–35, 15:9–12, New Life

What would you find if you took personal inventory based on these words of Jesus? Would you see the flame of Christ's love burning bright in your heart or dimly flickering? Would you be experiencing fullness of joy? Depending on your answer, it may be time to evaluate your love walk. Just because we experience God's love and just because He placed His love within us, doesn't mean it's vibrant in our daily lives. If we love others, we won't gossip about them or entertain anger or envy. We'll be quick to forgive and serve one another.

Unconditional love *begins* with our horizontal relationship with our brothers and sisters in Christ. Paul reaffirms this in his first letter to the Thessalonians: "But concerning brotherly love [for all other Christians], you have no need to have anyone write you, for you yourselves have been [personally] taught by God to love one another" (1 Thess. 4:9, AMP).

We might as well be on the level—sometimes it isn't easy to love fellow believers as Christ loves us. Yet, that is what God requires, and that's what the world expects of us, too. People hear Christians talk about the love of Christ, but they don't see some of us showing it. Often we hear them saying, "Why would we consider becoming Christians when they are not any different than us?"

History contains evidence of those who bore the name "Christian"; yet they harbored prejudice, hatred, and even waged war against one another. And I'm sorry to say it even happens in our current day and age. How this must hurt the heart of God.

John, known as the apostle of love, shows how an intimate relationship with God and perfect love are inseparable: "My beloved friends, let us continue to love each other since love comes from God. Everyone who loves is born of God and experiences a relationship with God. *The person who refuses to love doesn't know the first thing about God, because God is love—so you can't know him if you don't love"* (1 John 4:7–8, THE MESSAGE, emphasis added). According to

> If we love others, we won't gossip about them or entertain anger or envy. We'll be quick to forgive and serve one another.

John, there is no gray area—it's black and white. He doesn't leave it to interpretation. If you know God, you desire to love; if you refuse to love, you don't know God. This is another area where it comes down to a matter of the heart. When we show the unconditional love of Christ to our brothers and sisters, a far different story unfolds. The world takes notice, the Gospel becomes energized, and the Spirit of God changes lives.

LOVE—FEAR'S ANTIDOTE

The threat of terrorism, natural disasters, nuclear holocausts, economic uncertainties, and increasing crime are just a few of many reasons for the rise in fear in our world today. Multitudes are in therapy and take medications for various fear-induced physical and psychological disorders. The Bible confirms the tormenting effects of fear but also provides the antidote—God's perfect (unconditional) love.

> There is no room in love for fear. Well-formed love banishes fear. Since fear is crippling, a fearful life—fear of death, fear of judgment—is one not yet fully formed in love.
>
> —1 JOHN 4:18, THE MESSAGE

The answer to fear is so simple, yet some people are willing to try anything else before they consider the power of God's unconditional love as revealed in His Word. His love dispels the fear of rejection, condemnation, bondage, punishment, abuse, failure, abandonment, harm, lack, and even the greatest fear—death. The atoning sacrifice of Jesus Christ on the cross accomplished this, whereby, as the Bible states, He "crushed the serpent's head." (See Genesis 3:15.) The following scripture shows that Jesus broke the power of fear that held sway over the human race because of death's grasp: "Jesus took on a flesh and blood body that through His atoning death he would destroy the devil's hold on death; And deliver those who through fear of death were subject to bondage all their lifetime" (Heb. 2:14–15, author's paraphrase).

ALL YOU NEED IS...TOLERANCE?

The world has created its own pseudo-version of love. It's nothing more than mental consent, which makes a person feel good but ultimately lacks substance. Great strides have occurred to remove prejudice, which is rooted in love's opposite—hatred—from our societal consciousness. However, unfortunately, it's still alive. If you read between the lines of the media, you can readily see it hidden in the guise of "tolerance." Some might say, "Now, just wait one minute. Shouldn't we show tolerance to everyone and live in harmony, regardless of race, religion, and gender?" My response is yes, we should; but let me give you an example to explain my thoughts.

Suppose you ask me, "How are you and your wife doing?" and I respond with, "I'm tolerating her." You would probably conclude that we didn't have a very good relationship—and rightly so. But if I responded with, "I love her more now than when I first married her thirty-six years ago," you would think our marriage was great (and, by the way, this statement is true).

Do you see that it's possible to tolerate someone but still not love them? You can recognize and respect their rights or beliefs, yet harbor hatred for them in your heart. We cannot make a genuine, lasting difference in the lives of those we merely tolerate. Jesus never asked His followers to *tolerate* one another but

> The Bible confirms the tormenting effects of fear but also provides the antidote—God's perfect (unconditional) love.

love one another. The scripture doesn't say, "God so *tolerated* the world that He gave His only begotten Son." It says, "God so *loved* the world that He gave His only begotten Son." Aren't you glad that God doesn't just tolerate us but *loves* us? That is why only the pure, selfless, *agapē* love of Christ can give hope and bring healing to our world. It doesn't see color, creed, or social status but the inherent value that God places on every human being.

LOVED DESPITE OURSELVES

Big-Hearted People demonstrate unconditional love to others. But what does it really mean to love unconditionally? French novelist, poet, and artist Victor Hugo described it perfectly: "The greatest happiness of life is the conviction that we are loved—loved for ourselves, or rather, loved in spite of ourselves."[2] Take a moment and read this quote again slowly. This, my friends, is the essence of unconditional love. I believe there's not one person on the planet who doesn't want the assurance that they are loved despite themselves. This all-consuming love views the object of its love as worthy. It doesn't look for anything that merits love. There is no *quid pro quo* or need to reciprocate. The lover shows love regardless and doesn't need to receive anything in return. This is the highest form of love and the kind we experience from God.

God showed His unconditional love for us through the cross of Jesus Christ. There has never been or will ever be a demonstration of greater love. Let your imagination follow me back to Jerusalem during the reign of Tiberius Caesar Augustus and his governor, Pontius Pilate. Amid the throngs of people, we direct our eyes to a hill called Golgotha, located outside the ancient city. There we see three men crucified—two of them thieves. Between them hangs the broken, bloody body of an innocent victim dying for the sins of humanity—and the same ones who nailed Him to a tree. A cruel crown of thorns, fashioned to mock this lowly King of the Jews, tenaciously pierces His head. Others ridicule and taunt Him as He dies. Heartless soldiers laugh as they throw dice to win His only garment. Lifting His head and gazing toward heaven He cries out, "Father, forgive them; for they know not what they do" (Luke 23:34, KJV).

The sinless one pardons the sinner; the guiltless one acquits the guilty; the lovely one forgives the unlovely. Jesus' single act proved the truth about what He spoke in His Sermon on the Mount:

> You have heard that it has been said, 'You must love your neighbor and hate those who hate you.' But I tell you, *love those who hate you.* (Respect and give thanks for those who say bad things to you. Do good to those who hate you.) *Pray for those who do bad things to you and who make it hard for you* ... If you love those who love you, what reward can you expect from that? Do not even the tax gatherers do that? If you greet only the people you like, are you doing any more than others? The people who do not know God do that much.
> —MATTHEW 5:43–44, 46–48, NEW LIFE

A HUNK OF BURNING LOVE

It's easy to love those who love us; the previous words of Jesus echo the obvious. But how do we treat people in the everyday course of our lives? How do we react if someone cuts us off in traffic or takes advantage of us? What do we say to the person who speaks an unkind word or slanders us behind our back? The world says, "Don't get mad; get even"—I hardly see the difference. The mistaken notion that revenge is sweet is the current trend in many movies. The bad guys do something evil to the "good" guy, his friends, or family, and the rest of the story follows a pattern of revenge. Of course, the "good" guy eventually gets even in a violent way and satisfies his thirst for revenge. How…entertaining? Yet in stark contrast, God's Word flies in the face of the world's ways.

> If it is possible, as far as it depends on you, live at peace with everyone. Do not take revenge, my friends, but leave room for God's wrath, for it is written: "It is mine to avenge; I will repay," says the Lord. On the contrary: "If your enemy is hungry, feed him; if he is thirsty, give him something to drink. In doing this, you will heap burning coals on his head." Do not be overcome by evil, but overcome evil with good.
>
> —ROMANS 12:18–21, NIV

When we respond in love to those who wrong us, they don't know how to respond. They're probably shocked because that's not the way it happens in the world. They have no weapon to use against us anymore—they're made powerless. That's what it means when the scripture speaks figuratively: "You will heap burning coals on his head" (Rom. 12:20). Often, God will ask us to do something kind for someone we don't especially care for—that one person who just rubs us the wrong way. He will want us to ask forgiveness from them for anger or resentment we have held against them—even if they're in the wrong! Why would He ask us to do something that doesn't make sense and "goes against our grain"? Because God knows that His love never fails—that's right, never—and He wants us to experience this truth ourselves.

Now to be honest, at times I still find this difficult. In my heart, I want to be like Jesus when it comes to blessing those who wrong me or loving the unlovely, and I'm making ground by God's grace. I'm farther along than I was a few years ago, but it's not an easy road—for anyone. Maybe that's where you are as well. I have found that it takes more than a solid determination, more than a resolute act, more than trying to do better. These are merely works of our fallen human nature and will end in failure. It takes complete cooperation with the Holy Spirit to bear the love-fruit that God requires. It's a step by step process. As we respond to others according to the Word of God, we will start to see not only a change in them but also a change in us. We will know the truth that love never fails, not only according to our understanding but by experience.

LOVE ME TENDER?

Though the emphasis in this chapter is mostly on unconditional love, a balanced love walk is vital for Big-Hearted People. Figuratively speaking, God's perfect love is like a multifaceted diamond—it is not one-dimensional. It always shines, though sometimes differently, depending on which facet reflects His light. The well-known love chapter of the Bible, 1 Corinthians 13, highlights these facets. Love is: patient, kind, content, humble, polite, selfless, peaceful, forgiving, truthful, trusting, hopeful, persevering, just, faithful, believing.

Yet some people carry the mistaken impression that love consists of warm, fuzzy feelings or gushing sentimentality. Maybe these false notions stem from dreamy, idealistic Hollywood movies. Well, love is blind, or at least it looks the other way—right? If it seems blind or looks the other way, it's because it has made the choice to do so. When God views us, His redeemed children, He does not look at our sin. He chooses to forgive and not remember our transgressions solely on the merits of Christ's blood and His imparted righteousness. The apostle Peter described the power of love when he told us, "Above all things have intense and unfailing love for one another, for love covers a multitude of sins [forgives and disregards the offenses of others]" (1 Pet. 4:8, AMP).

> The sinless one pardons the sinner; the guiltless one acquits the guilty; the lovely one forgives the unlovely.

God's love is not blind but sees clearly and always has the best intentions for the objects of His love. Though often love must respond in a way that seems to contradict its nature. The common phrase we use for this is "tough love."

Let me describe this using a practical example. If a physician discovers an invasive growth that threatens a patient's physical well-being, he may recommend surgery. This might include procedures that often result in pain and physical distress. Once the patient undergoes surgery, there's usually a required time for the body to recover and heal. All this is necessary so the patient can return to a normal, healthy lifestyle. But what if the patient became angry with the surgeon because of the resulting pain and discomfort? Most people would consider them foolish or, at best, ungrateful. Why? Because the surgeon did whatever he thought was necessary to restore the patient's health and maybe even prevent death. His decisions and actions always considered the best interests of the one under his care. As Big-Hearted People, we sometimes may need to show tough love—and it can cause pain. If this is the case, our actions must always lead to restoration and healing.

As many of you know all too well, raising teenagers can be painful and difficult for both the parents and teens. Crises happen because the teens are making the transition from childhood to adulthood. Physical, emotional, and spiritual changes occur, and their peers often wield more influence than their parents.

Allow me to share a personal experience that may help me get the point across. Years ago, one of my daughters did something that required us to discipline her. It was around this time that her school was having its homecoming celebration, and she anxiously anticipated attending. My wife and I decided to ground her from this event, hoping she would realize the severity of her disobedience. It wasn't an easy decision, and it caused us hurt to see her disappointed. Well, she was angrier than she was disappointed and let me know by saying that she hated me. In my heart, I knew she didn't mean it, but I had to stand firm with the decision to ground her. She learned through the experience that Mom and Dad loved her deeply. After a few more bumps in the road of life, she finally reached adulthood. Our daughter is married now with children of her own, and she disciplines them in love as well.

> As Big-Hearted People, we sometimes may need to show tough love—and it can cause pain. If this is the case, our actions must always lead to restoration and healing.

Occasionally God shows love to us through discipline because we are His children.

> Or have you forgotten how good parents treat children, and that God regards you as his children? My dear child, don't shrug off God's discipline, but don't be crushed by it either. It's the child he loves that he disciplines; the child he embraces, he also corrects. God is educating you; that's why you must never drop out. He's treating you as dear children. This trouble you're in isn't punishment; it's training, the normal experience of children. Only irresponsible parents leave children to fend for themselves. Would you prefer an irresponsible God? We respect our own parents for training and not spoiling us, so why not embrace God's training so we can truly live? While we were children, our parents did what seemed best to them. But God is doing what is best for us, training us to live God's holy best. At the time, discipline isn't much fun. It always feels like it's going against the grain. Later, of course, it pays off handsomely, for it's the well-trained who find themselves mature in their relationship with God.
>
> —HEBREWS 12:5–11, THE MESSAGE

However, we need to realize that the chastisement we receive from God is not punishment because of our sins. God punished Jesus for our sins on the cross. Second Corinthians 5:21 explains, "God made Jesus who was without sin, to be a sin offering for us, so that in Him we might become the righteousness of God [in Him]" (author's paraphrase). In modern terms you could say that God's chastisement is a mid-course correction. This is His method of showing us that we are walking in disobedience. Our response should be to repent and rely on His grace to walk in a way that pleases Him. So, it's obvious that God's purpose in discipline is always for our best. I can readily speak from experience, having gone to God's "woodshed" many times.

We need God's guidance to know which facet of His love He wants us to reflect. Sometimes love must bend, but at other times it needs to be firm. Often it's necessary to temper love with justice. This is why it's so important for us to rely on God's wisdom in every circumstance. In the next chapter, I'll expound on how we can teach our spirits to discern God's voice and receive His wisdom.

7

SENSITIVITY TO PEOPLE'S NEEDS

Sensitivity: the awareness of the needs and emotions of others[1]

To begin this chapter, I will use an unusual example to introduce this attribute shown by Big-Hearted People. As you read on, my aim to describe this more effectively will become clear.

In keeping up with the need for precise global location information, improving destination accuracy, and reducing travel time, many employ the use of GPS receivers. These receivers communicate with the global positioning system, a constellation of twenty-four satellites that circle the globe and transmit precise timing signals. The GPS receiver is especially sensitive to transmitted signals through its antenna, which determines its location, direction, velocity, and time. However, the receiver is subject to limits because it can only do one thing—receive. It can never transmit. A transceiver is a different device that shares the common circuitry of both a transmitter and receiver. Thus, it not only receives but transmits as well.

God created you and me with the capacity to receive from and transmit to Him and each other. As complex beings with a body, soul, and spirit, we have been wired to facilitate communication in various ways. The quality of our reception however, directly correlates to our sensitivity. Are some people gifted with a unique inner-sensitivity to people's needs? How can we be receptive to God's voice and subsequently more sensitive to the needs of others? By closely examining this Big-Hearted attribute, we will discover answers to these questions.

Many Big-Hearted People have an uncanny ability to remember significant details about others. They remember people's names and faces, their likes and dislikes, birthdays, anniversaries and even special family celebrations. Usually, they're quick to notice something different about a person's appearance, possibly a new hairstyle or clothing, and will always offer a genuinely kind compliment. This is because they are people-persons—attentive listeners who make a point to store relevant data about others in their memory banks for later retrieval.

I believe that these folks have an easier time being sensitive to others because it's naturally resident in their soul. They're usually more sociable and apt to ask all kinds of questions about your life and about your family. It's not that they're nosy or trying to pry; they simply have a genuine interest in you as a person, an interest to learn what troubles you or what makes you happy. It's easy for them to encourage people with shut-up hearts to open up and enjoy life. Their antenna is always operating, so they can be more sensitive to receive even the weakest signals from their fellow humans. If you're happy, it brings a smile to their face. If they find you overburdened with troubles or with a pressing need, they will try to help you in any way possible. They won't rest until they're certain that you're doing well and satisfied because you no longer have a need.

> God created you and me with the capacity to receive from and transmit to Him and each other.

Do you know people like this? Perhaps this description applies to you. Or maybe you see your need to be more receptive and are looking for ways to improve your sensitivity. However, to be especially sensitive to others, we must learn to be sensitive to the Holy Spirit and His leading. So let's find out how.

THE SHEPHERD'S VOICE

The first thing we must understand is that God *wants* to teach us, lead us, and direct our lives. He makes it plain to us through His Word.

> I will instruct you and teach you in the way you should go; I will counsel you and watch over you.
>
> —PSALM 32:8, NIV

> For as many as are led by the Spirit of God, they are the sons of God.
>
> —ROMANS 8:14, KJV

Once we realize this, the next step is to discover how to listen for His voice. I'll explain by using my family as an illustration. God has blessed my wife and me with seven grandchildren, and we thoroughly enjoy every opportunity to babysit. We read stories to them, play games, and have a great time together. But no matter how much fun they're having with us, their little ears always expect to hear two familiar sounds. After the front door opens and they hear Mommy and Daddy's voices, they stop whatever they're doing and run to greet them. To these little ones, their parents' voices represent security, comfort, and love. They won't react with similar excitement by hearing the voice of any others—only Mommy and Daddy.

Why does this happen? I'm sure nobody has to tell you the answer, especially if you've raised children. Even after the first few minutes of a child's birth, the most familiar voices are already those of their parents. The baby has become familiar to the resonance of the mother's voice (and probably the father's) while still in the womb. As soon as a baby awakens in the morning, the first gentle words they hear are usually from Mommy. Then, if they're fortunate, they'll continue to hear them throughout the day. The last words they hear before closing their eyes at night are from Mommy, Daddy, and often, both. So by familiar example, we see that these little ones know their parents' voices *because they spend time with them.*

The tenth chapter of John's Gospel highlights a biblical parallel. However, instead of parents and children, we will focus on a shepherd and his sheep. Here Jesus shares a parable in which He describes Himself as the Good Shepherd and we as His sheep:

> "The sheep hear his voice; and he calls his own sheep by name and leads them out. And when he brings out his own sheep, he goes before them; and the sheep follow him, for they know his voice. Yet they will by no means follow a stranger, but will flee from him, for they do not know the voice of strangers. I am the good shepherd; and I know My sheep, and am known by My own."
>
> —JOHN 10:3–5, 14, NKJV

So clearly, because of our relationship with the Good Shepherd, the only way we can know His voice is to spend time with Him. Sadly, many of us spend more time with our televisions than we do with Jesus. Now, please don't think I'm saying that it's wrong to enjoy a good movie or TV program—it's not. I don't want you to feel condemned if you do. We simply need to make fellowship with Jesus our top priority so we can learn to tune our hearts to hear His voice. I believe that unless we do, we won't be as effective in showing Big-Heartedness to others.

When my three daughters were young, I asked them to ponder the following example to understand what it means to experience intimacy with Jesus. I told them, "Suppose a man and woman were on their honeymoon and the husband said to his wife, 'Sweetheart, I thought that after our honeymoon I would rent my own apartment, and you rent your own apartment too. Every weekend or so we can get together for a few hours and spend quality time together.' If his wife agreed, do you think they would experience an intimate relationship and have a good marriage?" My daughters would immediately answer, "No way!" "Similarly," I said, "if we don't regularly spend time with Jesus (more than just on Sunday morning), can we truthfully say that we have an intimate relationship with Him?" They clearly understood the point I was trying to make. It was a simple example meant to explain a deep truth. I will revisit this, but with more detail in chapter 16.

In the Old Testament we read about another shepherd—one who understood this through personal experience. Before David became the king of Israel, he was a lowly shepherd boy. No doubt, he spent many days in the wilderness with his flock of sheep, musical instrument, and his God. I can picture him gazing into the cloudless, coal black night sky laden with glittering stars. His heart fills with wonder at God's creation, and he takes up his harp to accompany his praise-filled voice. (Those who sing and play instruments can easily identify with David's passionate worship.) These times alone with God shaped

> So clearly, because of our relationship with the Good Shepherd, the only way we can know His voice is to spend time with Him.

David into what the Bible describes as "a man after God's own heart"—even despite his moral failures. If you study David's life, you encounter a recurring theme that confirms his intimacy with God—"and David inquired of the Lord." David realized that he had to seek God's guidance if he was to be successful. He resolved to make God's will first in his life.

Like David, if we are to be men and women after God's own heart, we must learn to be sensitive to His voice through seeking Him. In so doing, we will become sensitive to the needs of others because we can discern the heart of God. Personally, I would much rather trust the Lord to lead me than live only by my own senses and understanding. Considering this, the question of how God speaks to us may come to mind. That's certainly a legitimate response, and asking is the first step in finding the answer. To begin, I'll highlight a great example from the Old Testament.

THE GENTLE, QUIET WHISPER

The prophet Elijah discovered how to hear God's voice in a unique way. This scriptural account highlights Elijah's experience:

Then he was told, "Go, stand on the mountain at attention before God. God will pass by." A hurricane wind ripped through the mountains and shattered the rocks before God, but God wasn't to be found in the wind; after the wind an earthquake, but God wasn't in the earthquake; and after the earthquake fire, but God wasn't in the fire; and after the fire a gentle and quiet whisper.

—1 KINGS 19:11–12, THE MESSAGE

Elijah didn't find God in the powerful, earthly demonstrations but only as God's Spirit quietly whispered to his heart. We find that he immediately responded to the voice of God.

It's almost the same with us, but we have a distinct advantage—even over Elijah. The Spirit of God only came *upon* men and women before the outpouring of the Holy Spirit at Pentecost. We who have received salvation through the atoning sacrifice of Jesus Christ have the Holy Spirit dwelling *inside* us. He is always abiding within and will never leave us. He is the one whose gentle voice we hear. The Holy Spirit speaks to us by communicating with our spirit. (See Romans 8:16; 1 John 4:13.)

In the Book of Colossians, we find another way the Lord communicates with us: "Let the peace of Christ rule in your hearts, since as members of one body you were called to peace. And be thankful" (Col. 3:15, NIV). The word *rule* comes from the Greek word *brabeuō*, which means "to be an umpire—to decide, direct or control."[2] When we step out in faith, the Lord directs us by giving us His peace when we are on the right path. But if there is an absence of peace, or a check in our spirit, we should stop and wait or change direction. The more we

> The more we tune our hearts to listen and respond to God in obedience, the more God will use us to bless others.

tune our hearts to listen and respond to God in obedience, the more God will use us to bless others. If we are sensitive to the Holy Spirit, He will even help us to discern people's needs, though it might not be obvious to our senses. You will probably make some mistakes learning to hear God's voice—it happens to everyone—but God will redeem your mistakes.

Remember, our loving heavenly Father will always ask us to reach out with love and kindness, because that's His nature. He gently encourages and inspires and will never force us to do anything. Satan is the one who tries to force and drive us, because that's his nature. His purpose is to steal, kill, and destroy. But God will never ask us to do or say anything that will harm or injure anyone.

WHAT WOULD JESUS DO?

WWJD is a popular acronym that appeared on wristbands, T-shirts, and Bible covers a few years ago. It stands for "What would Jesus do?" When you think about it, ask yourself, Just what *did* Jesus do? The answer is simple. The Scriptures tell us He did everything His Father told Him. (See John 5:19.) Every circumstance was different; He asked the Father what to do and responded to His Father's will. He didn't heal people the same way every time. He didn't feed people the same way every time. He didn't pray for people the same way every time.

When you read Gospel accounts of Jesus healing the blind, He didn't use the same method. One time He made a paste of mud and placed it on the blind man's eyes. On another occasion, He just touched the eyes to restore sight. To heal blind Bartimaeus, Jesus merely spoke, "Go...your faith has healed you" (Mark 10:52, NIV). In each instance He did exactly what the Father told Him, and the results were always the same—*restoration*.

In like manner, we're to be attentive to the Holy Spirit to discern our Father's will and do what He asks. As humans and creatures of habit, we love following procedures, checklists, or prescribed formulas. It's so much easier that way. The same steps performed repeatedly can guarantee success every time—right? Not necessarily. Maybe that's the way it's done in the world, but not so in the kingdom of God. This is why it's so important to be sensitive to the Holy Spirit's leading in every different situation. So, the next time God's gentle voice prompts you to perform a kind deed for someone, act on it without hesitation. You will see how sowing a small act of Big-Heartedness may reap a great harvest of blessings.

Several years ago a friend at work shared with me that she was experiencing complications in her pregnancy. She was worried about her unborn child. At that moment, I sensed an urgent prompting of the Holy Spirit to pray for her. I asked her permission to pray, and she agreed. I told her to place her hand on her belly, and I placed my hand on hers. It was a while ago, so I don't remember the words of the brief prayer I prayed. I urged her to trust God for answering the prayer and tell me her progress. A short time passed, and when I saw her, she told me with much joy that the baby was doing much better.

Years later, my wife and I had the privilege of inviting my friend, her husband, and her healthy, intelligent young boy to our home for dinner. Yes, his birth came about with no problems because of God's faithfulness. Does this mean I will follow the same method once again if I pray for a pregnant woman? Probably not, because the Holy Spirit directed me to pray in that particular way one time only and not again since. So it's important that we ask the Lord to reveal His will in each situation and respond in obedience.

Jesus called us to be His representatives on the earth. He has placed the words of reconciliation in our mouth. Paul reaffirms this in his second letter to the church in Corinth: "We're Christ's representatives. God uses us to persuade men and women to drop their differences and enter God's work of making things right between them. We're speaking for Christ himself now: Become friends with God; he's already a friend with you" (2 Cor. 5:20, THE MESSAGE). Looking at this in another way, when we are sensitive to people's needs this is what happens: we become Jesus' hands as we reach out to people. We become His eyes of love when we look at others. Our feet carry us wherever God leads us to show compassion. I have summed up this chapter and shaped it in the form of a poem. Allow me to share this with you.

THE ONLY JESUS PEOPLE WILL SEE

Have you ever thought that people,
Who deeply need to know the Lord,
Would really believe God exists,
If His audible voice they heard?

Or maybe they would worship Him,
If a miracle were performed,
Or perhaps repent of their sins,
If by a spirit they were warned?

But those aren't the things God uses,
According to the Bible's view,
To show His love to a lost world,
His perfect plan is using you.

Or perhaps a fellow Christian,
In the midst of a fiery trial,
Who needs to hear a word from God,
Or a touch and a gentle smile.

The Lord is reaching out in love,
With comforting peace to imbue,
But to help His hurting children,
His perfect plan is using you.

Your own hands are His extended,
You walk to do good as He walked,
His words are spoken with your voice,
In love and kindness like He talked.

He hugs the lonely with your arms,
While giving hope to the forlorn,
You see their heartaches with His eyes,
His tears mingle with those who mourn.

So let Him pour His love through you,
Then you will know with certainty,
You reflect the only Jesus,
That people's eyes will ever see.

—R. J. SCHUM

Part II

GUIDING PRINCIPLES FOR BIG-HEARTED PEOPLE

Big-Hearted People are always looking for ways to improve. They're dissatis-fied with the status quo when it concerns their walk with God and relationship with people. It's with this in mind that I define guiding principles that will help us be more effective as Big-Hearted People. Maybe you are already familiar with some or all of them. If that's the case, then I'll reiterate the words of the apostle Peter: "For this reason I will not be negligent to remind you always of these things, though you know and are established in the present truth" (2 Pet. 1:12, NKJV).

No matter how you view these principles, my purpose is to reveal what God's Word has to say about them. I'll show you their practical application in daily life. But understanding something with our mind is only the first step. We must get the Word into our hearts before it can begin to take effect. In this way, it becomes resident in our spirit—something like a spiritual second nature—which bears eternal fruit. I will further discuss how we can accom-plish this throughout Part II of this book.

The apostle Paul writes to the church in Philippi using a descriptive word that shows us one way to apply these principles: "Whatever you have learned or received or heard from me, or seen in me—put it into practice. And the God of peace will be with you" (Phil. 4:9, NIV). Paul is telling them to practice what they have learned—the same way we need to approach it. Years ago, I read a book titled *The Practice of the Presence of God* by Brother Lawrence, a seventeenth-century French monk. It's a short book of less than seventy pages, but its simple message highlights an extraordinary truth. By regular practice, Brother Lawrence learned to experience intimate communion with God and the overwhelming joy of His presence—continually. With his example in mind, *practicing* simply means to take what we've learned from the Holy Spirit and God's Word and walk it out in our daily lives.

However, some people might still view these principles as lofty ideals, and to be honest, they are. If you think you can just buckle down and try to do better using your own strength and wisdom, you'll not succeed. You must realize that it's something you can't perform on your own. However, when you step out in faith, God will enable you with His wisdom, strength, and power to put them into practice. Once you understand that there's no need to strive or strain, you'll experience a peace that transcends your understanding.

I can't describe it more beautifully than Jesus does, as He offers us a choice to surrender our striving in exchange for a wonderful promise of rest. The modern language of *The Message* Bible makes it easy to understand: "Are you tired? Worn out? Burned out on religion? Come to me. Get away with me and you'll recover your life. I'll show you how to take a real rest. Walk with me and work with me—watch how I do it. Learn the unforced rhythms of grace. I won't lay anything heavy or ill-fitting on you. Keep company with me and you'll learn to live freely and lightly" (Matt. 11:28–30, THE MESSAGE). Consider the relevancy of these words in this particular time in history. Can you imagine if people took this to heart? They'd experience abundant peace, robust health, and have less need for psychological counseling and medications. Yet we will begin to experience these added benefits as we daily practice the principles I set forth in the following chapters. So let us keep Jesus' timely words before us as we travel the path on the second part of our sojourn.

8

THE HEALING POWER
OF FORGIVENESS

Humanity is never so beautiful as when praying
for forgiveness or else forgiving another.

—JEAN PAUL RICHTER[1]

Forgiveness is essential if Big-Hearted attributes can become fully alive and work in us effectually. On a personal level, our body, soul, and spirit can experience great harm by holding on to unforgiveness, resentment, or bitterness. If we're not vigilant, these can easily become the heaviest burdens we carry.

Medical science has discovered a direct connection between unforgiveness and some cancers. In his book *What You Don't Know May Be Killing You,* Dr. Don Colbert gives credibility to this statement. He says:

> Deadly emotions wreak havoc on our physical bodies. I would consider bitterness, resentment and unforgiveness to be three of the most deadly emotions a person can have. These emotions may actually prevent the body from releasing toxic material, especially from the liver and gallbladder. This buildup of toxins in the system can eventually lead to disease. Before I treat a person with cancer, I encourage that person to release any anger, bitterness or resentment that may be harbored inside through the power of forgiveness....I have found that my patients are often unable to receive their healing until they release these deadly emotions....The excessive stress caused by negative emotions is quite dangerous because it increases our cortisol levels, which then suppresses the immune system.

When the immune system is suppressed, cancerous cells can begin to form and grow.[2]

At its most extreme, unforgiveness—resulting in bitterness—can eventually lead to death if not dealt with. Some of us still carry deep emotional wounds and personal pain because of things done to us in the past. Possibly, we carry guilt or shame for things we have done to others. These can impede the flow of the Holy Spirit in and through us. We must deal with the spiritual aspects of forgiveness before we can expect any healing to occur in our lives.

Unforgiveness is like a cork in a bottle. It prevents God from pouring out His blessings on us—and through us to others. The Book of Hebrews describes the result of harboring bitterness: "Pursue peace with all people, and holiness, without which no one will see the Lord: looking carefully lest anyone fall short of the grace of God; lest any root of bitterness springing up cause trouble, and by this many become defiled" (Heb. 12:14–15, NKJV). This root, left unchecked, can grow just like spiritual cancer. Underneath the surface it spreads its deadly tentacles until it defiles the whole being.

As deep-rooted unforgiveness can defile and destroy us, then the opposite must be true. Living a life of forgiveness can promote physical, emotional, and spiritual health. Forgiveness opens the door of healing to others as well as ourselves. It helps us process the wounds and pain we have experienced in our lives. That's why I chose to title this chapter "The Healing Power of Forgiveness." As a Big-Hearted Person, you'll find that people will hurt you. It's certain. They might misunderstand your Big-Hearted acts, and you could even face rejection. Some people may try to take advantage of you. That's why forgiveness is so important if we are to live a life of Big-Heartedness. Jesus spoke strongly about the need to forgive. Let's take some time to learn from the one who taught us forgiveness by His Word and through His example.

REPAIRING BROKEN BRIDGES

Most if not all of us can recite the Lord's Prayer by memory. When we look closely at the words of this prayer, the importance of forgiveness becomes plain. We also discover that it's conditional as well.

And forgive us our debts [sins], as we forgive our debtors [those who sin against us]. And lead us not into temptation, but deliver us from evil: For thine is the kingdom, and the power, and the glory, for ever. Amen. [*Immediately* after reciting the Lord's Prayer, Jesus reemphasizes the condition related to God's forgiveness.] For if ye forgive men their trespasses [sins against you], your heavenly Father will also forgive you: But if ye forgive not men their trespasses, neither will your Father forgive your trespasses [sins against Him].

—MATTHEW 6:12–15, KJV

It's simple to understand. Forgive and you will receive forgiveness; don't forgive and you will not receive forgiveness. I am fully aware of my need for God's forgiveness—on a regular basis. Therefore, I don't want anything in my life that prevents God from showing His goodness to me or showing it through me to others.

Maybe the first person you need to forgive is yourself. I know this because I have dealt with it in my own life. Perfectionism is what drives us to be too hard on ourselves. Failure is not an option for the perfectionist. Perhaps, like me, you've said to yourself, "I should've known better," or, "I can't believe I let that happen," or, "I'll never do that again." What we need is a realistic view of ourselves. We are fallible and need forgiveness. God is infallible and plentiful in mercy and grace. Sometimes we fall short of God's best for us, and it results in sin. We should immediately turn to God, confess it, ask His forgiveness, and let it go. We can't do anything to earn it. He forgives us because He loves us. Once we receive His forgiveness, we can begin to forgive ourselves.

> Living a life of forgiveness can promote physical, emotional, and spiritual health. It opens the door of healing to others as well as ourselves.

THE UNFORGIVING SERVANT

How often should we forgive someone, especially if they wronged us? Once? Twice? Many times? This question was in Peter's mind, too. Peter went to Him and asked, "Lord, how often shall my brother sin against me, and I forgive him? Up to seven times?" (Matt. 18:21, NKJV). Peter probably thought seven times was being more than generous. Jesus said to him, "I do not say to you, up to seven times, but up to seventy times seven" (v. 22, NKJV). Then Jesus expounded by sharing this parable:

> Therefore the kingdom of heaven is like a certain king who wanted to settle accounts with his servants. And when he had begun to

settle accounts, one was brought to him who owed him ten thousand talents. But as he was not able to pay, his master commanded
that he be sold, with his wife and children and all that he had, and
that payment be made.

—MATTHEW 18:23–25, NKJV

Note the failure to pay his great debt would have resulted in slavery for
him and his family. And this comes as no surprise, since Proverbs warns that
"rich people rule over poor people, and the borrower is servant [or slave] to the
lender" (Prov. 22:7, author's paraphrase).

The servant therefore fell down before him, saying, 'Master, have
patience with me, and I will pay you all.' Then the master of that
servant was moved with compassion, released him, and forgave him
the debt. "But that servant went out and found one of his fellow
servants who owed him a hundred denarii; and he laid hands on
him and took him by the throat, saying, 'Pay me what you owe!'
So his fellow servant fell down at his feet and begged him, saying,
'Have patience with me, and I will pay you all.' And he would not,
but went and threw him into prison till he should pay the debt. So
when his fellow servants saw what had been done, they were very
grieved, and came and told their master all that had been done.
Then his master, after he had called him, said to him, 'You wicked
servant! I forgave you all that debt because you begged me. Should
you not also have had compassion on your fellow servant, just as I
had pity on you?' And his master was angry, and delivered him to
the *torturers* until he should pay all that was due to him. "So My
heavenly Father also will do to you if each of you, from his heart,
does not forgive his brother his trespasses."

—MATTHEW 18:26–35, NKJV

What may not be obvious is the relative value of the money the servant owed
to the master—and how much the servant's debtor owed. The servant's debt
calculates to about ten million dollars. He could never pay that debt. The total
owed to the servant was less than one hundred dollars. With this in mind,
when we look into our hearts, we realize that we could never pay the enormous
sin debt we owe to God.

As Jesus hung on a cross between two thieves, He forgave those who mocked,
abused, scourged, and crucified Him when He cried out, "Father, forgive them,

for they know not what they do." Jesus paid the sin-debt of humanity in full through the cross. He forgave us completely, and the Bible states that "He remembers our sin no more" (Heb. 10:17, author's paraphrase). From Jesus' example, we see that forgiveness does not denote weakness but strength. When we ask God to forgive us, we find that His forgiveness sets us free from guilt and condemnation. It doesn't matter how many times in a day we ask Him to forgive us because He doesn't take count. First John 1:9 states, "If we [freely] admit that we have sinned and confess our sins, He is faithful and just (true to His own nature and promises) and will forgive our sins [dismiss our lawlessness] and [continuously] cleanse us from all unrighteousness [everything not in conformity to His will in purpose, thought, and action]" (AMP). However, God does expect us to deal with besetting sins so we can live before Him and others with purity of heart.

THE SPIRITUALLY HEALTHY CHOICE

Now that we know what God's Word says about His willingness to forgive us, shouldn't we make the choice to forgive those who wronged us or ask forgiveness from those we wronged? You may be thinking, "That's easy for you to say, but they are not sorry" or "they don't deserve forgiveness" or "you don't know what they did to me" or "they won't accept my forgiveness."

To be truthful, it doesn't matter. God first asks us to forgive, regardless. I've heard many people say, "But I don't feel like forgiving." Well, if you wait until you feel like it, you never will. Others might say, "I can't forgive." Are you saying that you can't forgive because you refuse to, or is it because you realize you

> Maybe the first person you need to forgive is yourself.

can't forgive in your own strength? The often-used phrase "to err is human, to forgive divine" is more true than some people realize. It must be a supernatural work of God's grace within us to forgive, but we have a free will to make that choice. God will never force us.

You see, forgiveness is a matter of two things—an act of the will, and an act of faith. You must decide to come before God in prayer, maybe like this:

> *Dear Lord, I don't feel like forgiving. You already know what's in my heart, but I make the choice by faith and in obedience to Your Word, and I forgive _____ for what they did to me. I ask You to forgive*

them too and bless them, so they also may experience your love and
forgiveness.

You may pray that prayer when all the while you are gritting your teeth and
your stomach is churning. Yet, if you prayed in faith God will, in His own way
and time, turn it around for good. (See Romans 8:28.) Sometimes immediately
or as time progresses, you will begin to experience inner freedom. Your feelings will come in line with God's love, which passes all understanding. You'll
begin to feel mercy and compassion toward that person where there was once
bitterness and hatred.

Sometimes we come to realize there are many people we need to forgive.
Recently, I was speaking to a friend who admitted that he has held on to bitterness toward many people for years and years. This continued to build until it
was finally taking a physical and emotional toll. I suggested the only way to
know freedom was to forgive all the people who hurt him. I urged him to go
to a quiet place with pen and paper and make a list of everyone who has ever
wronged him. I went on to explain that once he had the list, he was to bring it
to the Lord in prayer. Each one he had identified, he must forgive. The same is
true for you. Say, "Lord, I forgive," and speak their name. Only then will you
experience a deliverance from your problems.

Maybe you're hurting on the inside because of what someone did to you. Only
you have the ability to remove the hurt—and that is by forgiving. However, you
might need someone to help you walk the road of forgiveness, and that's where
members of the body of Christ come in.

A PARTNER ON THE ROAD TO FORGIVENESS

With the rise in divorces and broken homes in our society, bitterness, anger, and
resentment are at an all-time high. I have witnessed this devastation firsthand
with family members and friends. To those who choose the path to forgiveness,
it may seem like a long, winding road with no end in sight. They realize that if
they're going to complete their journey they must have a Big-Hearted partner
who will walk with them—someone to help them receive a breakthrough. This
is certainly understandable, and God's Word highlights how important it is to
share the struggles and burdens of others.

> Those of us who are strong and able in the faith need to step in and
> lend a hand to those who falter, and not just do what is most conve-
> nient for us. Strength is for service, not status. Each one of us needs

to look after the good of the people around us, asking ourselves, "How can I help?" That's exactly what Jesus did. He didn't make it easy for himself by avoiding people's troubles, but waded right in and helped out. "I took on the troubles of the troubled," is the way Scripture puts it.

—ROMANS 15:1–3, THE MESSAGE

Some people have experienced such deep hurt or abuse that it's difficult for them to forgive, and their lives become ravaged because of it. On a practical level, the first step to freedom includes helping them to understand what the Bible says about:

- Why they must forgive
- Jesus' example of forgiveness
- Relying on God's grace *to forgive*
- The freedom of forgiveness

As they begin to realize their need to forgive, the Scriptures become the foundation for prayer. It is through prayer that you lead them to God's throne of grace to confess resentment and bitterness as sin. Prayer becomes the voice of forgiveness expressed toward the person who caused the pain or hurt. The release of spiritual power and freedom occurs when they speak the words rather than just think them in their mind. Giving voice declares sincerity, reaffirms a covenant relationship with God, and helps to free the soul from bondage.

> It must be a supernatural work of God's grace within us to forgive, but we have a free will to make that choice.

Walking down this road with others makes a difficult journey much easier because of the power of agreement between two believers and God's Word. It's one of the highest and most sacred privileges of a Big-Hearted Person.

WHAT'S LOVE GOT TO DO WITH IT?

Love motivates forgiveness. We see this confirmed in 1 Corinthians 13, where it says, "It keeps no record of wrongs" (v. 5, NIV). When someone says, "I can forgive, but I can't forget," then it's not forgiveness at all. Let's ponder Jesus' parable, covered earlier in this chapter. We see the master delivered the wicked servant to the torturers (or tormentors) because he refused to forgive. I believe that represents what happens to us when we refuse to forgive and hold resentment in our hearts. If we don't forgive, it binds us to the one who wronged us.

We will never get free of them or of the tormenting thoughts until we forgive. Do you realize the other person may be enjoying every day of their life, unaware that you harbor resentment against them? It's hurting you, not them.

Years ago, I remember hearing a story about how an ancient culture punished murderers. They tightly tied the body of the victim to the killer, so freeing himself from the corpse was impossible. They drove him out of the village, and after a few days, the decaying flesh of the victim started to spread corruption to the murderer's own flesh. He faced a slow, agonizing death. This is a perfect example of what happens to us spiritually when we don't forgive. It's like carrying a rotting corpse that can eventually destroy us.

That's the reason Jesus stressed the need for us to forgive. It's for our sake, so we can enjoy life because we are free from the bondage of unforgiveness. When we forgive, we let go of the past. We no longer think about or tell others what someone did or said to hurt us or how they abused or took advantage of us. We no longer want them to pay for what they did because we realize that God is our vindicator. (See Romans 12:19.)

The other reason Jesus urged us to forgive is to free the other person to *receive* forgiveness. They may, indeed, know what they did to hurt you and haven't even asked for forgiveness. But when you take the initiative to forgive, you set in motion the power to break the chains that hold them captive.

> If we don't forgive, it binds us to the one who wronged us.

However, sometimes people will not accept your forgiveness. If they don't, then it's not your matter anymore. You've done your part to forgive. Now, all you can do is pray for them to be receptive to God's forgiveness and yours. Pray and believe that love never fails, and simply trust God to soften their hearts.

There will be times when God will ask you to do something special and kind for the person you've forgiven. You might be thinking, "Aren't you taking this too far? It was hard enough for me to forgive this person; now I have to bless them as well?" Yes. But this simple act can change the life of someone who hasn't accepted your forgiveness. It can transform their hard heart into a tender heart. (Do you remember Jesus' words about doing good to those who do bad things to you, which I wrote about in chapter 6?) This reminds me of the words of Mark Twain: "Forgiveness is the fragrance the violet sheds on the heel that has crushed it."[3]

Christians, who bear the testimony of being followers of Christ, should be the first ones to show love and forgiveness to one another and to people in the world. Sadly, this is not always the case. We still hear and read reports of Christians suing each other, bitter church divisions, and even abuse of various kinds. How much these actions differ from the words of Paul: "And become useful and helpful and kind to one another, tenderhearted (compassionate, understanding, loving-hearted), forgiving one another [readily and freely], as God in Christ forgave you" (Eph. 4:32, AMP). The Amplified Bible accurately expounds on the way Christians should interact with each other. Just imagine what would happen if husbands, wives, and children would practice this at home. Domestic violence, divorces, and substance abuse incidents would dramatically decline. We'd see far less trouble in our schools, and families would experience renewed physical and emotional health. For the world to understand and receive God's forgiveness, they must first see this displayed in us. May we as God's people ask Him to manifest the grace of forgiveness in our everyday lives.

Once we are free from unforgiveness (a major hindrance to Big-Heartedness) we can show kindness, empathy, compassion, and love, especially toward those who are suffering or have desperate needs. Why? Simply because forgiveness can free us to become *selfless* instead of *self-focused*. The healing power and freedom that come with forgiveness is the way we show God's love to a world desperately in need.

THE FREEDOM OF SIMPLICITY

*Purity and simplicity are the two wings with which man
soars above the earth and all temporary nature.*

—Thomas à Kempis[1]

The Beauty of a Simple Life

Simplicity can bring peace and contentment to our lives wherever it is applied—in commerce, the arts, religion, technology, and even relationships. Yet, the greatest benefit is that simplicity releases us to become Big-Hearted to others by living a life of quality instead of quantity. That's why I view simplicity as a heart matter, because that's where it begins.

I have studied the life of St. Francis of Assisi (1181–1226) and marveled at how God used this humble man to carry out His will. Francis came from a wealthy family but instead chose to live simply to serve God and his fellow man. He regarded material possessions as of little worth and had a great concern for the needs of others ahead of his own. He viewed everyone as bearing God's image and worthy of love and acceptance. Francis was able to see beauty where others could not because he saw with his heart. This gentle man was content in his relationship with God. Therefore, he became a yielded vessel through which God showed His love and compassion. His life typified Big-Heartedness.

The beauty and splendor of God's creation was a constant source of amazement to him. He possessed a childlike wonder of the world and all that it contained. He recognized the glory of God in the simplest of creatures. Francis considered the birds of the air and animals of the forest his friends. In his song "Canticle of the Sun" (originally "Canticle of the Creatures"), he praises God the Creator for Brother Sun and Sister Moon, Brother Wind and Sister

Earth, and for all they give us. Francis's marked simplicity is evident in this well-known poem "The Peace Prayer," which has inspired people for centuries. Though read and enjoyed by many, I wonder how much we understand and how often we experience the truth it reveals.

Take a few moments to read these words from "The Peace Prayer" slowly and prayerfully. Ask God to help you become a Big-Hearted instrument of His peace.

> Lord, make me an instrument of your peace;
> Where there is hatred, let me sow love;
> Where there is injury, pardon;
> Where there is doubt, faith;
> Where there is despair, hope;
> Where there is darkness, light;
> And where there is sadness, joy.
>
> O Divine Master,
> Grant that I may not so much seek
> To be consoled as to console;
> To be understood, as to understand;
> To be loved, as to love.
>
> For it is in giving that we receive;
> It is in pardoning that we are pardoned;
> And it is in dying that we are born to eternal life. Amen.[2]

THE KINDEST CUT OF ALL

As I mention in another chapter, my dad was a farmer. He possessed an intimate understanding of the principle of sowing and reaping. He knew the value of pruning his plants and trees at the proper time. He taught me about two basic cuts—thinning and topping. By these methods, you remove dead or diseased branches and trim excess growth. My dad also told me about other nonproductive shoots or branches; he called them "suckers"—although living, they produce nothing. They take the vital nourishment the plant could use to otherwise stimulate growth and bring forth abundant fruit. Yet pruning seems so drastic. You wonder if the plant will survive after cutting off much of its growth. Then something astounding happens. Hidden from sight, the roots dig deep into the soil, drawing up the nourishment needed to sustain life. The bud appears, and then the blade of the leaf. The early fruit grows to maturation, producing a bountiful harvest. Surely this is one of God's simple miracles!

Likewise, we need to do some pruning in our own lives. Though we won't notice the growth as dramatically as the previous example, it can still yield a great harvest. As we submit to the Holy Spirit, He reveals areas in our life that are nonproductive, hinder our growth, or prevent us from producing fruit. We then make the choice to "prune" our lives as necessary to encourage new growth and yield lasting fruit that glorifies God. This form of pruning helps us to experience the freedom of simplicity.

I believe there are two areas where we can allow simplicity to take root and flourish in our lives. The first is spiritual, the life of the soul and spirit. The second is practical, the life consisting of our relationships with others, the things we need to live, and those that give us pleasure.

HAPPY DAYS

"Sometimes I wish life wasn't so complicated and would just slow down; I'm so weary and frustrated." Maybe you've heard these words spoken by someone, or perhaps you've spoken them yourself. We live in a fast-paced world where multitasking is one of the methods we use to cope with our hurried lifestyles. But does that make it better? Despite modern inventions intended to provide an easier life with time for recreation, we actually have less time and more stress. Peace and contentment seems more like an impossible dream than a realistic goal.

> As we submit to the Holy Spirit, He reveals areas in our life that are nonproductive, hinder our growth, or prevent us from producing fruit.

Do you remember television programs like *Leave It to Beaver*, *The Andy Griffith Show*, and *Little House on the Prairie*? Some folks view these shows as quaint, naïve, and maybe even boring, yet there's something unique about these people and their lifestyles that can't escape our attention. What can it be? A quality that we wish for but often eludes our experience, and that's simplicity. I'm not saying their lives were easier, but rather simpler—and that makes all the difference.

The hustle and bustle of daily life often makes us yearn for the simple bygone days. However, if we don't change our lifestyles now, we might discover the future looking the same or worse. In a few years, we could even view the stress-filled days in which we currently live as the "good old days"—and that's a scary notion.

I once saw a bumper sticker that made me laugh, but it contained an unintended element of truth. It read, "Jesus is coming soon. Look busy." There are multitudes of well-intentioned people who think that serving God is all about being busy. You know what I mean, "religious" busy. If they're not, God is not happy with them—or so they think. The distinct message I'm trying to convey through this book is this: it's the ordinary, simple things we do for others that make a difference. This is what brings joy to God's heart, not our busyness.

One of Satan's tactics to prevent us from producing fruit is to keep us preoccupied with busyness. He knows that it distracts us from what's important in life. Satan doesn't mind if we're even doing good things, just as long as it isn't what God wants us to do. Human nature always has a tendency to make life complicated, and Satan is glad to help. The Bible warns us that the way he chooses to deceive is to corrupt our minds from the simplicity of Christ.

> But I fear, lest somehow, as the serpent deceived Eve by his craftiness, so your minds may be corrupted from the simplicity that is in Christ.
>
> —2 Corinthians 11:3, nkjv

In my early twenties, I was experiencing health problems related to stress. I decided to talk to my pastor hoping he had insight through which he could offer me some helpful advice. He looked at me intently but with kindness in his eyes said, "You are so busy working and preparing for tomorrow, you are not enjoying today." I pulled a note from my pocket and answered him, "But you don't understand. I have so much to do that I need to write it down. Look at my list!" He asked to see it and said, "Let's look at the items on your list to decide how urgent they are."

We reviewed them one by one, and when we finished I finally understood what he meant. I discovered that I could postpone what I thought was important and necessary or remove it altogether—and without a negative impact. Once I saw that it was nagging duties that made my life more complicated, I chose simplicity. I felt like a weight lifted from my shoulders. Not only did I experience the freedom of simplicity, but I gained valuable insight as well.

When we bring simplicity into our plans, it allows us to be flexible, especially about the Lord's will. It also saves us much grief. But after we experience simplicity, we should occasionally take personal inventory to prevent ourselves from drifting back into a complex lifestyle. It sneaks up so subtly that if we're not vigilant, we'll fall right back into bondage. I have found the best way to sustain simplicity is to constantly remind myself of what God's Word has to say about it.

SINGLE-MINDED AND LOVING IT

Probably the most misunderstood Being in the universe is God. He is far greater and more complex than our minds can grasp. Yet He reveals Himself to mankind in a simple way so we can understand His nature. So often we are the ones who make life complex. We think that He wants so much from us. But in truth, He just wants us to know and enjoy Him in simplicity. God never intended for us to live complicated lives. Neither does He want us to become "weary in well doing" (Gal. 6:9). So just how should we order our lives so simplicity takes priority? The answer—change our focus through the lens of God's Word. The Scriptures use different phrases: "undivided heart," "single hearted," "single-minded," and even "double-minded." Each provides a gem of truth. However, no matter how we see them used in the Bible, they all still point to the benefits of simplicity. Digging deeper into God's Word will help us uncover some of these treasures.

> One of Satan's tactics to prevent us from producing fruit is to keep us preoccupied with busyness.

The Greek word for "simplicity" is *haplotēs,* which means "singleness, simplicity, sincerity, mental honesty—not self seeking, openness of heart manifesting itself by generosity."[3]

We see it used in Romans 12:8: "He that giveth, let him do it with simplicity; he that ruleth, with diligence; he that sheweth mercy, with cheerfulness" (KJV). Surprisingly, we find this same Greek word used in Colossians 3:22 and translated as "singleness of heart": "Servants, obey in all things your masters according to the flesh; not with eyeservice, as menpleasers; but in singleness of heart, fearing God" (KJV). Another Greek word, *aperispastōs,* translated "undivided," carries a meaning similar to "simplicity." It means "without distraction, without solicitude [concern] or anxiety or care."[4]

Think about it: How do you picture a Christian who is without distraction and has no concerns, anxieties, or cares? I see someone at peace, content, and experiencing great joy. I imagine a person not prevented in giving time and resources to glorify God by serving others. Why? Because of an undivided heart, he or she does not become bogged down with the affairs of life. I'm not saying that arriving at this place is easy, but I know that with God's help it is possible.

David, the king and Old Testament psalmist, also realized his need for an undivided heart. You can almost sense the urgency of his prayer as he entreats God: "Teach me your way, O LORD, and I will walk in your truth; give me an undivided heart, that I may fear your name" (Ps. 86:11, NIV). First Corinthians describes it as an intense focus or purpose: "I am saying this for your own good, not to restrict you, but that you may live in a right way in undivided devotion to the Lord" (1 Cor. 7:35, NIV).

The likeness of these verses reveals that simplicity can take root and grow in single, undivided hearts and minds. The apostle James reveals the same truth but from the opposite perspective. He addresses Christians and tells them to avoid double-mindedness.

> ...he who doubts is like a wave of the sea driven and tossed by the wind. For let not that man suppose that he will receive anything from the Lord; *he is a double-minded* man, unstable in all his ways.
>
> —JAMES 1:6–8, NKJV, author's emphasis

Probably most of us have experienced double-mindedness at one time or another. We make up our minds about something and then change it a few more times before settling on a final decision. I have—and truthfully there were times I felt as if I were quadruple-minded! We will never receive from God if we are anything more than single-minded, and I speak from experience. (I guess this shoots down the so-called efficiency of multitasking.)

Have you ever told a child you would do something special for them? They simply believe that you will do what you say, and they show excitement as if you've already done it. This is the same faith based on simplicity that God wants us to exercise: "Lord, you said you would do it in your Word, so I stand on your promise and believe that it's done." Then we go our way rejoicing because the answer is on its way.

However, double-mindedness taken to the extreme can result in severe consequences. Jesus addressed this when he spoke to the church in Laodicea—and it's not a pretty picture:

> "I know your deeds, that you are neither cold nor hot. I wish you were either one or the other! So, because you are lukewarm—neither hot nor cold—I am about to spit you out of my mouth. You say, 'I am rich; I have acquired wealth and do not need a thing.' But you do not realize that you are wretched, pitiful, poor, blind and naked."
>
> —REVELATION 3:15–17, NIV

Jesus was inferring that being lukewarm was the same as being double-minded in their devotion to Him. It seems the Laodiceans wanted Him, but they wanted the world also. Scriptures like this underscore how important God views simplicity, especially in our walk with Him.

SPIRITUAL SIMPLICITY

You've probably heard the good news of God's Word referred to as "the simple gospel." That's because simplicity is the foundation of God's reaching out to mankind. Jesus came to Earth to preach His simple message to the common folk. He told us to become like children (sincere, humble, trusting, teachable, simple) if we want to see the kingdom of heaven. (See Luke 18:16.)

When we come to Christ, spiritual simplicity first reveals itself in the knowledge that God calls us His beloved. As living branches, we draw nourishment from abiding in Jesus—the Vine. As His sheep we find contentment with Jesus—the Good Shepherd. There is a peaceful rest that accompanies our lives when we experience this truth. We find that we don't have to strive or wonder if we are in the center of God's will. When you look at it closely, what God wants from us is simple: "He has shown you, O man, what is good; And what does the LORD require of you But to do justly, To love mercy, And to walk humbly with your God?" (Micah 6:8, NKJV).

Often, we make our relationship with God far more complex than He intends for us. We think we should always be doing something considered "spiritual." So we attend church, read our Bibles, pray, and perform other acts of religious service. While spiritually important, they fall short unless we first enjoy intimacy with Jesus. The Lord hasn't called us to do, but to be:

- His child
- His bride
- His friend
- His servant
- His chosen one
- A sheep of His pasture.

Think closely at what each of these means to us—and to God.

Intimacy with God begins by listening to our hearts and responding. The Bible confirms this in the Book of Galatians: "And because you are sons, God has sent forth the Spirit of His Son into your hearts, crying out, 'Abba, Father!'" (Gal. 4:6, NKJV).

The word *abba* stems from an Aramaic origin and translates as "papa" or, in the endearing term familiar to us, "daddy." There's only one recorded instance where Jesus used this word to address His Father. We read this account of Jesus in the garden of Gethsemane.

> He went a little farther, and fell on the ground, and prayed that if it were possible, the hour might pass from Him. And He said, "Abba, Father, all things are possible for You. Take this cup away from Me; nevertheless, not what I will, but what You will."
> —MARK 14:35–36, NKJV

One can almost sense His desperate heart's cry. Like a child who's being separated from a parent, he pleads, "Daddy, if it's possible, don't let this happen to me." Jesus' intimacy with His Father was His deepest desire, so much that He sweated drops of blood when He faced only a temporary separation from Him. This separation took place the next day as Jesus was dying on the cross when He cried out, "My God, my God, why have you forsaken me?" (Mark 15:34, NIV). His Father turned away His face from Him—He could not look upon Jesus as He bore the sins of mankind. May this help us to understand how deep and intimate our relationship should be with our heavenly Father as well.

Simplicity can take root and grow in single, undivided hearts and minds.

The Lord delights to have us come before Him in simplicity to praise, worship, and thank Him for His goodness and blessings. Yet, sometimes our fellowship with the Lord consists of simply being quiet and still before Him.

Now, maybe it's hard for you to carve out time in your busy schedule to fellowship with the Lord. If that's the case, then you're just too busy. Guys, if a friend asks you to come over to his house and watch the playoffs, you'll make time to do it. Ladies, what would you do if your sister told you about a big sale at the downtown clothing store? No doubt you would spend a few hours to go shopping with her. We can always find time for the things we really want to do. It's all about priorities. This is just another reason we may need to simplify our lives.

We should also carry simplicity into our prayer life. It amuses me when I hear people pray using big words with theatrical voices. It's almost as if they think their eloquence somehow attracts God's attention. In truth, the prayer that God responds to is the simple prayer of faith. It's not the *words* but the *faith* that becomes the substance of things hoped for. (See Hebrews 11:1.) That's why

He told us to be like little children. Can you imagine a child coming before his mother and saying, "I beseech thee, O gracious and kind mother, who through wisdom and goodness takes care of my daily needs. I come before you humbly and without guile. Though I am most unworthy, please grant now my request to receive a cookie for dessert."

It's humorous to think that any child would ask for a cookie using that language. Most kids would say, "Mommy, can I have a cookie, please?" Mom's immediate response would be to give her child what he or she asks for—with pleasure. This is how we should view the willingness of God to answer our simple prayers. Sometimes "Lord help me" is enough to cause God to act on our behalf according to our faith. When Jesus' disciples asked Him to teach them to pray, He taught them the Our Father, a simple prayer that gets God's attention.

Practical Simplicity

As a young boy, if I wanted to have the latest toy or game, I wouldn't always get it. After hearing the word no from my parents a few times, I changed my thinking. I determined the only way to have a similar substitute was to make it myself or ask my dad to make it for me. My friends had store-bought authentic-looking toy rifles that made shooting sounds. Mine was wooden and simple, but I didn't care. It shot rubber bands and brought me pleasure. During my early teen years, my friend's parents bought them factory-built motorized minibikes. My mom and dad couldn't afford to buy one, so I built one using bicycle parts, an old engine, and a makeshift clutch. It wasn't sleek like my friend's minibikes and was simple—but it worked fine. As an added benefit, I gained valuable problem-solving skills that helped me with future challenges. Through these and other similar experiences, I learned about practical simplicity at a young age.

> Intimacy with God begins by listening to our hearts and responding.

"Live simply, that others may simply live."[5] This well-known phrase spoken by Mohandas Gandhi is no stranger to most of us. Can you imagine if everyone on the planet took this literally? I know what you're thinking—it will never happen—and you're right.

Yet, a disparity exists in our world that leaves Big-Hearted People unsettled: many people have little and few people have much. This is not what God intended for mankind. With this in mind, we can make the choice to simplify our lives enough to free us to show Big-Heartedness. Now, I don't support wealth redistribution as suggested by Socialism. I'm also not proposing that Christians should move to the country, dwell in communes, and live off the land. (Human nature always takes things to the extremes doesn't it?) Although, with the undesirable events that usually go with big cities, simple country living becomes tempting to say the least.

We can practice simplicity in every area of our lives. It all comes down to distinguishing between our wants and our needs. We reveal our priorities by how we spend our resources. Sometimes all it takes is evaluating what is most important to us and choosing to prioritize. God is not against us owning possessions as long as they don't own us. He just wants us to live *balanced* lives. Nineteenth-century preacher Jean Baptiste Henri Lacordaire viewed simplicity in this way: "What our age wants the most, is the sight of a man, who might possess everything, being yet willingly contented with little. For my own part, humanly speaking, I wish for nothing. *A great soul in a small house is the idea which has always touched me more than any other.*"[6]

As a homeowner, I occasionally accumulated broken items or ones that outlived their usefulness. I gathered them and took a trip to the local junk-yard. As I unloaded my truck, I looked around and saw broken, unusable remnants of what once were someone's precious possessions. Ruined remains of cars, boats, furniture, electronic gadgets, and appliances were clearly visible. Possibly, people made personal sacrifices to own them.

In hindsight, that experience gave me a sobering dose of reality and reminded me of what's really important in life. It made me take a personal inventory to see what I was sacrificing to obtain "wants." Have you ever held a garage sale? It's certainly a great eye-opener to see items that once cost dollars selling for just a few cents. Although, that's one way to receive a good lesson and make money at the same time!

The words of Jesus in Matthew's Gospel directly describe the kind of treasure we are to collect:

> "Do not gather and heap up and store up for yourselves treasures on earth, where moth and rust and worm consume and destroy, and where thieves break through and steal. But gather and heap up and store for yourselves treasures in heaven, where neither moth nor rust nor worm consume and destroy, and where thieves do not break through and steal; For where your treasure is, there will your heart be also.... But seek (aim at and strive after) first of all His

kingdom and His righteousness (His way of doing and being right), and then all these things taken together will be given you besides.

—MATTHEW 6:19–21, 33, AMP

The Apostle Paul also placed simplicity in perspective in his letter to Timothy: "A devout life does bring wealth, but it's the rich simplicity of being yourself before God. Since we entered the world penniless and will leave it penniless, if we have bread on the table and shoes on our feet, that's enough" (1 Tim. 6:6–8, THE MESSAGE).

After raising two of our three children to adulthood, my wife and I decided to downsize to a new home. We were able to unload some unneeded possessions that we had collected over the years. The freedom we received by relieving ourselves of unnecessary possessions was invigorating. Since then we have reduced our household inventory even more. When we finally move into our "retirement" home, we plan to live a simpler lifestyle. This will enable us to focus on what we consider more valuable.

I would never suggest that this, in some way, is a pattern for others to follow. Each of us must make our own decisions about what we think represents simplicity. However, in our fifty-plus years of living, my wife and I discovered the best things in life are not things at all! So if you have a loving family, close friends, and good health, you can consider yourself truly blessed.

Now some may think when we chose to live a simple lifestyle we somehow rack up points with God and become more pleasing to Him. Those notions are ridiculous! We please Him just as we are—in Christ. We must base any choice we make to simplify our lives on this alone, to free ourselves from anything that weighs us down and prevents us from serving God and others with joy. May our goal be to daily experience the freedom of simplicity.

I have chosen to use one of my sonnets as a bridge for your travel between "The Freedom of Simplicity" and "The Riches of Contentment." Written as a prayer, it addresses our gracious Lord who created everything. Its simple message can inspire our souls to reach beyond the superficial and focus on what matters most.

Sonnet VII

Greet Me with the Dawn

Greet me with the dawn; let my eyes behold
The exquisite wonders your hands have wrought.
May all the moments spent in quiet, unfold
The secrets of your world, so I am taught
To hold all earthly goods with open hands
And teach my soul to always be aware
Of all that's around me; to understand
How to spend each hour not in haste or care;
To choose the simple things in life, above
Anxious thoughts that would rob my soul of peace;
To savor the swift days with those I love,
So I may see familial joys increase
Before the long night is gathered, and I
Exhale—bidding mortality good-bye.

—R. J. Schum

THE RICHES OF CONTENTMENT

*Not that I am implying that I was in any personal want, for
I have learned how to be content (satisfied to the point where
I am not disturbed or disquieted) in whatever state I am.*

—PAUL OF TARSUS
PHILIPPIANS 4:11, AMP

HOW NOW, BROWN COW?

I just finished my afternoon meeting with the mayor of Orlando, Florida, to whom I made a proposal to perform a freelance artwork service for the city. After leaving his office, I walked toward the glass doors that opened into a large foyer. A chime tone signaled the elevator's arrival when it reached my floor. As the sleek, stainless steel doors slowly spread apart, I surprisingly beheld a beautiful, brown jersey cow lumbering out. Following closely was a distinguished-looking entourage. She (it was a female, trust me) was adorned with an ornate red cape inscribed with her name. A lovely floral wreath of bright yellow daisies graced her neck. Her horns, though uniquely shaped and shiny, were not any more stunning than her manicured hooves, which had a spit-polish shine. After a few minutes of amazement, I recognized that it was a photo opportunity for the Borden Company and their well-known bovine mascot, "Elsie."

Now, stick with me here. I *really do* have a point to emphasize.

For those of you old enough to remember the TV and magazine ads for Borden's condensed milk, it typically included the slogan "The milk from contented cows." It always amused me. I thought it was merely an advertising phrase hoping to conjure up some idealistic country scene in consumers' imaginations, inspiring them to buy their products. However, on researching this I discovered there is a thread of truth to the contented cow story. I heard about a dairy farm that employs a unique approach to improve the yield of milk production. By placing speakers in the barns and playing classical music, the annual milk yield has dramatically increased—much to the delight of the dairy farmers. Extraordinary! (It confirms the positive effects of classical music, too!)

If even milk cows will be more productive when content, what insight can we gain from this? Do you think it's possible, that we—made in God's image and more valuable to Him than cows—can become more effective in serving, more fruitful in showing kindness and Big-Heartedness, if we also are inwardly content? Let's take a closer look at this word *contentment,* one that seems archaic in our world of materialistic excess.

One would think that those who live in America, the most blessed, prosperous nation in history, should be the most content people on Earth. After all, the United States Constitution guarantees unparalleled liberties. Every citizen can enjoy peace and freedom, and many families live the American dream. Yet sad to say, many people still are not content. They're constantly searching for anything to make them feel happy and fulfilled. Some have gained enormous wealth, fame, success, and great power, but contentment still eludes them. The daily news media often reports on people who achieved great prosperity. Yet they suffer from depression, emotional instability, and broken relationships. Some have even committed suicide. It is not surprising, but despite all the evidence, people continue to pursue things that will never satisfy.

> Nothing that you or I can do, experience, buy, or obtain through any means other than God can make us content.

Nothing that you or I can do, experience, buy, or obtain through any means other than God can make us content. Why? Because we cannot have real contentment or true satisfaction until we experience a relationship with God through Jesus Christ. He is the one who loves us just as we are, the one who fulfills us and longs to have intimate communion with us. If we find ourselves discontent, we need only to look inside our hearts to evaluate our real focus and identify the sources that rob us of contentment.

To Have—But Not to Hold

I enjoy playing acoustic stringed instruments (guitar and renaissance lute) and creating calligraphy. Apart from the pleasure I receive, I've discovered something that helps me perform both with a greater degree of skill. Whether I play my instruments or hold my calligraphy pens, I must do so with the lightest touch possible. This cancels any tension and enables me to perform with a graceful, rhythmic movement. Otherwise, my muscles tighten and reduce the quality of the music or art.

Figuratively speaking, we need to hold on to the things we own in a similar fashion—lightly and with open hands. We should enjoy them while they're in our possession but not create inner tension within our souls by holding them too tightly or by worrying about their loss or having to give them away. Thomas Aquinas's words of wisdom from the thirteenth century are still relevant today: "Man should not consider his outward possessions as his own, but as common to all, so as to share them without hesitation when others are in need."[1] His words parallel the Book of Acts, where we read: "Now the company of believers was of one heart and soul, and not one of them claimed that anything which he possessed was [exclusively] his own, but everything they had was in common and for the use of all" (Acts 4:32, AMP).

God wants us to enjoy a life of fullness and blessing as long as He remains our central focus and the recognized Source of all that we have or are. Once this becomes our inner attitude, we can say with a thankful heart, "I am content with whatever I have because Jesus said He would never leave or abandon me." (See Hebrew 13:5.)

Contentment doesn't come by having everything you want but by being thankful for what you already have. It brings with it a wonderful freedom and is also the cure for coveting, which the Bible states is the same as idolatry. (See Colossians 3:5.) In the twelfth chapter of Luke, Jesus spoke to His disciples and the crowds gathered before Him:

> And He said to them, Guard yourselves and keep free from all covetousness (the immoderate desire for wealth, the greedy longing to have more); for a man's life does not consist in and is not derived from possessing overflowing abundance or that which is over and above his needs.
>
> —LUKE 12:15, AMP

Our possessions and riches can subtly draw our attention away from God and others. It doesn't happen overnight. If we are not careful, they will overtake us, little by little, and then shackle us to this world's system. I'm convinced the excessive craving for the things of this world is merely a symptom of the soul's distress—a heart issue. In the least, it's a case of distorted priorities.

A passage of Scripture that can open the eyes of our understanding is 1 John 2:15–17: "Don't love the world's ways. Don't love the world's goods. Love of the world squeezes out love for the Father. Practically everything that goes on in the world—wanting your own way, wanting everything for yourself, wanting to appear important—has nothing to do with the Father. It just isolates you from him. The world and all its wanting, wanting, wanting is on the way out—but whoever does what God wants is set for eternity" (THE MESSAGE). "Set for eternity"—I like that! Realistically, you'd think this would be easy; just watch what the world does and do the opposite. Yet the pull of the world is strong. We must make daily choices to be content and trust God's enabling grace to make it happen in our lives.

GETTIN' SOME SATISFACTION

Have you ever dined at a restaurant where the meal was not only delicious but also satisfying? Maybe the server came up to you and asked, "Is there anything else I can bring to you, possibly one of our desserts?" Smiling, you answer, "No thanks, the meal was great. I'm good." You're full, you're satisfied, you don't need anything, you're content. Now, wait a couple of weeks. Your mind begins to think about how much you enjoyed that dining experience. Your body begins to crave that delightful food once again. Before you know it, you're driving to the restaurant hoping to repeat your previous experience.

> I'm convinced the excessive craving for the things of this world is merely a symptom of the soul's distress—a heart issue.

What happened? You've gone from contentment to discontentment in just a few days. You based the experience on being full and satisfied. Once you became hungry, your body became dissatisfied. Normal experience, wouldn't you agree? Here's my point. As long as you are full of something that satisfies, you don't need anything else. Similarly, as long as we allow God to "full-*fill*" us, we will find complete satisfaction in Him. Let's take this to a higher level and look at it from a different vantage point.

A suitable description of the word *contentment* is "satisfaction with what you have and who you are as a person and not wanting to amass more possessions or become someone other than yourself." Do you notice that contentment is not only satisfaction with what you have but also with who you are? Please let me explain.

We should always be content with who we are because that's the way God made us, but we should not be content to remain as we are. Phillips Brooks, nineteenth-century minister and author, supports these thoughts. He wrote, "Sad will be the day for any man when he becomes contented with the thoughts he is thinking and the deeds he is doing—where there is not forever beating at the doors of his soul some great desire to do something larger, which he knows he was meant and made to do."[2]

The preceding statements may seem contradicting—be content but don't be content. However, a simple explanation will suffice. Although we should be content with who we are, we should still improve ourselves spirit, soul, and body. This is how we fulfill our dreams and God's plan for our lives. Biblical contentment does not suggest passivity but activity. The Scriptures confirm this by encouraging us to always move forward and grow in our knowledge and relationship with Jesus.

> That you may walk (live and conduct yourselves) in a manner worthy of the Lord, fully pleasing to Him and desiring to please Him in all things, bearing fruit in every good work and steadily growing and increasing in and by the knowledge of God [with fuller, deeper, and clearer insight, acquaintance, and recognition].[We pray] that you may be invigorated and strengthened with all power according to the might of His glory, [to exercise] every kind of endurance and patience (perseverance and forbearance) with joy.
>
> —COLOSSIANS 1:10–11, AMP

> But grow in grace (undeserved favor, spiritual strength) and recognition and knowledge and understanding of our Lord and Savior Jesus Christ (the Messiah).
>
> —2 PETER 3:18, AMP

Do you know people discontent with who they are? Maybe you're struggling with this in your own life. Often this stems from a dysfunctional relationship with parents, relatives, or friends. Some people never received affirmation of their value as a child or perhaps received unfavorable comparisons to siblings or others. They derive their expectation and worth from people instead of God. In the workplace, I've observed those who desperately strive for success, power, and recognition. The ironic result is that achievement in itself does not produce contentment or fill the void in the person's heart.

For many years, I struggled with feeling discontent about who I was as a person. I constantly tried to perform things to gain recognition. I thought it would make me feel good about myself—but it didn't. It wasn't until I began to view myself as God sees me, with love and acceptance, that I experienced a life-altering transformation. How did I begin to change the way I saw myself? I studied God's Word and began believing what He said about me (and it's what He says about *all* His children).

> Everything that we have—right thinking and right living, a clean slate and a fresh start—comes from God by way of Jesus Christ.
> —1 CORINTHIANS 1:30, THE MESSAGE

> Long before he [God] laid down earth's foundations, he had us in mind, had settled on us as the focus of his love, to be made whole and holy by his love. Long, long ago he decided to adopt us into his family through Jesus Christ. (What pleasure he took in planning this!) He wanted us to enter into the celebration of his lavish gift-giving by the hand of his beloved Son.
> —EPHESIANS 1:4–6, THE MESSAGE

> For we are God's workmanship, created in Christ Jesus to do good works, which God prepared in advance for us to do.
> —EPHESIANS 2:10, NIV

I realized that my identity was in Christ, who alone is good, perfect, and righteous. Once I stopped striving, I entered His rest and experienced a real freedom by not feeling compelled to do anything to impress anyone.

THE CROWN OF A CONTENTED HEART

True contentment is not dependent on external things—possessions, people, or circumstances. It finds rest solely in the heart. Even William Shakespeare recognized contentment as a heart matter. In his play *Henry VI*, Part III, we find the king roaming through the country. Approached by two gamekeepers, he tells them that he's a king. One of them asks him, "But, if thou be a king, where is thy crown?" His answer may surprise you.

> My crown is in my heart, not on my head;
> Not deck'd with diamonds and Indian stones,
> Nor to be seen: my crown is call'd content[ment]:
> A crown it is that seldom kings enjoy.[3]

Usually when you think of what a king's crown represents, you imagine power, wealth, majesty, and authority. Yet Shakespeare's King Henry realized his true crown was in his heart, and that crown was contentment. A Latin phrase of which I am fond is *Omnia mea mecum porto*. Translated, it means, "All that is mine, I carry with me." In other words, all that is important to me is within my heart; that is my greatest wealth. As Christians we carry our greatest treasure in our hearts—Jesus Christ, in the person of the Holy Spirit. Those whose hearts are content experience great riches indeed.

THE ALL-SUFFICIENT ONE

Most Christians and Jews are familiar with the often-recited pastoral Psalm 23, by the beloved psalmist and king of Israel, David. It begins with the phrase, "The LORD is my shepherd; I shall not want." Now, take a moment, speak this aloud slowly, and think about the magnitude of what you're saying.

> The LORD *[the almighty, all-sufficient God]* is my shepherd; *[because of this]* I will not *[lack for anything]* want *[so I am content]*.

Say it again. As you speak, does your heart bear witness to what these words infer?

One of the Judaic names of God is *El Shaddai*, "the all-sufficient God." The word *shad* means "breast" in Hebrew. If considered in a more familiar way, it reveals the tender side of God as our all-sufficient provider. A woman's breast produces the source of nourishment for her child. Have you personally experienced this or watched the act of breastfeeding? You cannot help notice the calm, almost surreal contentment of the infant. The baby seems relaxed, comfortable, and receiving all that he or she needs at that moment; there is no striving, no worry—all is well.

As Christians we carry our greatest treasure in our hearts—Jesus Christ, in the person of the Holy Spirit.

I vividly remember when my children were infants. All it took was for the baby to cry, and my wife's body would react to those cries. Immediately, she was ready and able to satisfy our child's hunger. As many times as the baby needed feeding, she was there to satisfy. That is precisely how we can view God's willingness to meet our needs. The scripture declares, "He knows exactly what we need even before we ask Him!" (Matt. 6:8, author's paraphrase). To take that a step further, He not only knows but also has *already provided the answer* before we ask Him. We simply ask in faith, believe that we receive, and then thank Him that it's done.

THE CHILDREN'S BREAD

A pastor friend of mine related a story to me that illustrates peaceful contentment through the assurance of bountiful provisions. After World War II, the Allied armies began to gather multitudes of homeless, hungry children and move them to camps. There they received tender care and generous portions of food. However, at night they slept poorly. Finally, a psychologist tried something with the hope that it could solve the children's sleeplessness. Upon going to bed, each child received a slice of bread but was told not to eat it—only *hold it.* The results were astonishing. The children would fall asleep subconsciously believing they would have something to eat the next day. This alone provided enough certainty to enable them to have calm and peaceful rest. As we hold on to God's promise of provision, we too can sleep soundly, content in the comfort that Jesus is our Provider.

ABUNDANTLY DISCONTENT

The Old Testament records a detailed history of God's chosen people, Israel. After their miraculous deliverance from Egypt, they journeyed to the Promised Land. This sojourn should have only taken them eleven days, but because of their hard-hearted unbelief, it became a forty-year trek. Despite God's tender care and His unfailing provisions, the Bible states that they provoked Him.

When they murmured about not having enough water, God supernaturally provided. When they complained about not having bread, He supplied heavenly manna (which foreshadowed Christ, the Bread of Life). They grew weary of eating manna and cried out for meat. God provided quails, and they gorged themselves until they became sick. They were neither thankful nor content, though God always met their needs. The Book of Hebrews warns us not to follow their example of murmuring, complaining, and unbelief.

As Christians, we have a blessed privilege to rely on the sure promises of God. He will always take care of us and provide our every need. In over thirty-eight years of employment at various companies, I've been laid off several times due to sluggish sales and downsizing. During these trials of faith, my heart constantly reminded me of the shepherd–king of Israel, David, who said, "I have been young, and now I am old. Yet I have never seen the man who is right with God left alone, or his children begging for bread. All day long he is kind and lets others use what he has. And his children make him happy" (Ps. 37:25–26, NEW LIFE).

Not once did my family suffer lack. God showed His faithfulness on our behalf despite our circumstances. Through these experiences, I learned that I would rather have His promise of full provision than millions of dollars in the bank. Why? Because money can't guarantee contentment, but God's Word can. Money can fail, but God never fails. The world boasts of self-sufficiency, but the Christian boasts of God's sufficiency.

~~I Did It My Way~~
I Do It Your Way

Are you still content when you discover that God's will crosses yours—or when it seems like He prolongs an answer to your prayer? Oops, I think I just hit a nerve. Are you starting to wince? Just stay with me here. You'll feel better; trust me.

God wants us to experience the riches of contentment. And through Him we can know deep contentment regardless of our circumstances or what's taking place in our lives, though I know it's much easier to talk about it than live it— but that's where we need to be. Isaiah tries to help us parallel our understanding of contentment with God's Word: "For my thoughts are not your thoughts, neither are your ways my ways," declares the LORD. As the heavens are higher than the earth, so are my ways higher than your ways and my thoughts than your thoughts" (Isa. 55:8–9, NIV).

We make plans, we develop agendas, we orchestrate and mastermind; but do we submit it all to His lordship? I'm learning to do this because I've tried doing it my way many times, became frustrated, and failed. Frustration comes when we try to perform something in our own strength or manipulate and control the outcome ourselves. Yet once we let go and let God, His perfect peace enters and frustration exits. Some people learn through teaching and some through positive experiences, but some learn by mistakes. I've learned by the latter more times than I care to recall. Though surprisingly, I'm glad, because He is showing me that His way is the only way that leads to peace and contentment. There was a time when I used to say, "If it's gonna be, it's up to me," but after some hard lessons I've since rephrased it. Now, I say, "If it's gonna be, it's up to Thee, Lord." I have since made progress, and for that I am thankful.

I worked at a company where one of the common sayings was, "If you fail to plan, then you are planning to fail." This makes sense, especially in the business world. Even in our own lives, it is necessary—to a certain extent. However, when it comes to making plans for my life and my family, God has taught me to indeed plan but also to go with *His* flow.

Rarely have my plans come about exactly as expected. (I can easily complicate matters.) By observation, I discovered that God's plan produced a far greater benefit. He also directed events in such a way that I clearly could see His divine purpose. Proverbs addresses this in plain language: "We humans keep brainstorming options and plans, but God's purpose prevails" (Prov. 19:21, THE MESSAGE).

Often we struggle with inner conflicts that we must resolve before we experience contentment. Let your mind's eye wander back two thousand years to the predawn hours on the Mount of Olives in a garden called Gethsemane. The flowing waters of the brook Kidron ripple like soothing music in the distance, but the sights and sounds at this hour are anything but serene.

A solitary man falls prostrate and pours out His heart to God. Hot tears caress His face and quickly disappear into His beard. Though innocent, he knows that He must suffer a criminal's death as a sinless human sacrifice, bearing the sins of mankind. In deep anguish of soul, His sweat mingles with tiny drops of blood. He faces humiliation,

> God wants us to experience the riches of contentment. And through Him we can know deep contentment regardless of our circumstances or what's taking place in our lives.

torture, and death—but that isn't the worst. In His most desperate hour, God will turn His face from Him and sever the intimacy they had always known. Jesus, the God-Man, struggles in His humanity until He surrenders Himself to His Father's will: "Father, if you are willing, please take this cup [of suffering] from me, nevertheless not my will but yours be done" (Luke 22:42, author's paraphrase).

I believe that despite what Jesus faced, once He prayed through and submitted His will to His Father, He became filled with contentment. Isaiah prophesied that the Messiah would "see the travail of His soul and be satisfied [content]" (Isa. 53:11). He experienced contentment because He implicitly trusted His Father's will over His own.

We will never experience the same physical, emotional, and spiritual suffering as Jesus. Yet He asks us to follow His example by submitting our will to the Father's so He can fulfill His divine purpose through us. From personal experience, I would rather trust my plans to an omniscient God than try to shape my life in my own way and face a less-than desirable (or even tragic) outcome.

"God is rarely early, but He is always on time." I heard this said years ago, and I have since repeated it in many conversations. These few words speak volumes. God is the Lord of time and eternity. He has synchronized the entire universe, timing it to the fraction of a second. He is the Beginning and the End, who upholds everything by the word of His power. Since God acts according to His own timetable, He doesn't need to consult us to ensure His schedule doesn't conflict with ours.

As human beings we want *what* we want, and we want it now! Advertisers are quick to seize on our weakness in this area. They tell us we can have it now, but they never show us the results of acting impulsively. To prove our impatient human nature, just observe a baby when he's hungry. He usually begins crying with just enough volume to tell you he wants food. If you don't respond right away, the crying gains in intensity and quickly becomes screaming. His face turns red. He may even start to shake and won't let you rest until you satisfy his hunger. That's how he communicates. He is hardwired to know how to get Mommy's and Daddy's attention.

> God is rarely early, but He is always on time.

Often we are much like that little infant, though less dramatic. In prayer, we ask God to meet certain needs or bring our plans to pass. As if He didn't already know, we explain all the details to Him, including our preferred schedule. He probably finds this amusing. However, He speaks to us through His Word and directly to our spirit, telling us to place everything in His hands and trust His timing.

The writer of Hebrews shows us that faith and patience go together: "Imitate those who through faith and patience inherit the promises" (Heb. 6:12, NKJV). Patience is what God uses to temper faith. If God immediately answered every prayer, it wouldn't take much faith to believe Him, would it? But when He prolongs the answer and we are *content* to wait until He provides in His own time, our faith becomes strengthened. In addition, we will receive God's best for us, and He will receive the most praise. Therefore, I believe God often waits until "a minute before midnight" to come through. I have experienced it time after time.

So often we wait and wait and it seems like nothing is happening. But He knows just what we need, and He knows exactly when we need it. I can assure you that when God is ready to bring the answer, nothing in heaven and on Earth will prevent Him from bursting forth suddenly—at just the right moment. By His grace, may we learn to be content not to know how and when He will meet our or others' needs but to simply rest in the truth that He will do so, indeed! As Big-Hearted People, we will experience the riches of contentment by patiently trusting God.

11

IT'S THE LITTLE THINGS

Little deeds of kindness, little words of love... Help
to make earth happy like the heaven above.

—JULIA FLETCHER CARNEY, NINETEENTH-CENTURY POET[1]

IT'S THE LITTLE THINGS

It's not performing mighty deeds,
That brings the most reward;
It's not great accomplishments, that
Our worth should underscore.

It's not one's noble achievements,
That deserve accolades;
Or by using special skills, that
Define us as self-made.

It really is the little things,
We do every day, to
Bless, and encourage others, and
Help them along life's way.

Maybe it's just a cheerful note,
Sent to a special friend;
Or preparing a home-cooked meal,
To someone who's shut-in.

Perhaps, take some senior folks out
To lunch and pay the bill;
Or give a gift to a neighbor,
To demonstrate goodwill.

Make a visit to one who's sick;
Bring them some chicken soup!
Or phone call to a distressed soul,
With words that heal and soothe.

Babysit for a single mom,
Give her a needed break;
Give to families in need and be,
A blessing for their sake.

Visit someone who is lonely,
And simply be their friend;
To the helpless be a person,
In whom they can depend.

So, if you are thinking that your
Accomplishments be few,
You are the greatest blessing by,
The little things you do.

—R. J. Schum

It seems as though nearly every day we hear about someone whose great accomplishments merit accolades and applause. The media is replete with stories about people held in great admiration who reach success that few achieve. We certainly can say much good about these individuals. Many are simply ordinary people who overcame great adversity and persevered despite hardships to reach a goal. Sometimes they display the tenacity and raw courage needed just to survive. They are the ones who can serve as role models and inspire us to achieve in ways we never thought were possible.

Yet sometimes our focus is on the prestige, honor, and celebrity that often accompanies what some consider great achievements. Because of this, we lose sight of the small acts of Big-Heartedness that may not be as notable in the eyes of many yet are far more important. Often it's not great achievements that make a difference in people's lives; it's the simple, little things. Usually these small acts happen in the background, without much notoriety and fanfare.

Does this mean they are less significant? Absolutely not! I believe small acts of Big-Heartedness often hold more value in God's eyes than great deeds recognized by the world. That's why we should never minimize the power of little things we do from day to day. Jesus Himself emphasized this when He told us, "And if anyone gives even a cup of cold water to one of these little ones because he is my disciple, I tell you the truth, he will certainly not lose his reward" (Matt. 10:42, NIV).

LEFT BEHIND TO MAKE A DIFFERENCE

Please allow me to share a personal example, one close to my heart. Six years after he was diagnosed with terminal cancer, my father said good-bye to his family and earthly home and entered his heavenly home. My mother was still heartbroken, even though she knew for months that his death was imminent. Nine months earlier, Mom and Dad celebrated their fiftieth wedding anniversary. They loved each other deeply and had never been apart from each other during all those years. Though God's comfort and peace sustained Mom, she still couldn't understand why God took him from her. I could only tell her not to try making sense out of it but just to trust God and allow Him to reveal the unexplained.

> Often it's not great achievements that make a difference in people's lives; it's the simple, little things.

Months later she emerged from her grief and moved on with her life. It was then that I began to see a pattern emerging. Everywhere she went, she greeted people with smiles, hugs, and shared the love of God and His goodness. Many people looked forward to her visits and kind, uplifting words. She reached out, befriended other widows, and encouraged them with hope. She was like a second mother to those whose parents died. Her family and friends were constantly the subjects of her prayers.

After a while, the answer she was looking for became clear. She discovered that, though a widow, God still had a special work for her to carry out in this life, one she had to do alone. We will never see her name listed in the *Who's Who of American Women* or hear that she won the Nobel Peace Prize. Yet she will receive a great reward by the Lord Jesus Christ because she was faithful in the little things, ones that made a significant difference in the lives of many people.

I could go on and on sharing examples from my own life and stories that friends and family shared with me, testimonies about how little acts of Big-

Heartedness resulted in a major blessing in someone's life. But now it's time to move on for some practical lessons.

GREEN ACRES UNIVERSITY

I was born and raised in upstate New York. My paternal ancestors made their living from the good earth as farmers, nurserymen, and landscapers. This continued until my generation, who then made the choice to follow other professions. Some of us soon discovered that although we made more money, our health and well-being were far less robust than our fathers. This showed us the health advantages of getting plenty of exercise and the accompanying peace that comes with working with nature.

Thankfully, when I was young boy, my dad taught me many valuable life lessons on the farm through examples from the flora and fauna. In one of Jesus' parables, He describes the miracle of reaping great things by sowing little things.

> The kingdom of heaven is like a mustard seed, which a man took and planted in his field. Though it is the smallest of all your seeds, yet when it grows, it is the largest of garden plants and becomes a tree, so that the birds of the air come and perch in its branches.
> —MATTHEW 13:31–32, NIV

Few individuals have the resources available to help people on a grand scale. However, we can use what we do have to bless others. Sowing little kindnesses can reap a great harvest. Not all of us can perform deeds that garner the praise of multitudes. Yet, all of us can look for little opportunities to make a difference in someone's life each day. I have seen where:

- a simple monetary gift enabled a friend to buy groceries and personal health products;
- a phone call provided hope and healing to someone in desperation because of marital conflicts;
- a young teen's life became transformed by an adult who reached out with love; and
- wise counsel about love and forgiveness prevented a divorce.

Performing little deeds is the place where Big-Heartedness starts. That is how faithfulness becomes established in our lives. Jesus emphasized the importance of faithfulness when He said, "He that is faithful with little things is faithful with big things also. He that is not honest with little things is not honest with big things" (Luke 16:10, NEW LIFE). God's plan is for us to be continually fruitful in everything we do. Faithfulness in small deeds opens the door for Him to perform big deeds through us.

SIMPLE GIFTS

You've heard it said, "Charity begins at home." Well, so does Big-Heartedness. We live so closely with our own family members that we often overlook opportunities to be patient and kind. Let's be the first to serve one another and be quick to forgive when someone speaks unkind words.

Try out these Big-Hearted ideas at home. Husbands, how would your wife react if you told her, "Honey, sit down and relax after dinner; I'll clean the table and do the dishes (or put them in the dishwasher)"? "Hey, guys don't do domestic chores!" would be the response I would get from most men. Men, just swallow your pride and do it anyway. You'll probably enjoy the response you will receive from your wife (after she gets over the shock).

> You've heard it said, "Charity begins at home." Well, so does Big-Heartedness.

Teens, if you're fortunate enough to have your grandparents still living, give them a phone call. Ask to spend some time with them. They will enjoy the opportunity to share stories about their life, possibly even stories you never knew about your parents! Dads, take your daughter out to dinner and go somewhere she considers special. The bonds you form will give her the security and confidence she needs to become a Big-Hearted woman someday.

If you're a senior citizen, volunteer to babysit for a single mom who hasn't had a night out in a long time. Perhaps you're a good cook. Create a special meal for someone who is sick at home. You may be a young parent. If so, visit a local assisted-living facility or nursing home. The residents will thoroughly enjoy your visit and love spending time with your children. You can also pick up inexpensive greeting cards for all occasions at a dollar store. Send them out to those whom you want to bless in a special way. Don't just sign the card. Write a personal message from your heart to theirs, one that will make their day. Think about the little things that people have done for you and do something special for them in return. If you are an employer, consider hiring disabled people. (Certainly, this depends on the severity of their disability). Many companies have discovered that they are hardworking and dedicated employees. Besides, it will give them a chance to become productive and independent members of society.

What about active listening? Yes, you read it right—*active listening.* I recently heard about a young man who placed an unusual ad on the World Wide Web. He posted his phone number and asked that if anyone wanted to talk to him, he would gladly listen. He literally received thousands of phone calls. So many people yearn for someone *just to listen* to them. When you sincerely listen to someone, it creates a feeling of caring. It helps to make the other person feel important and recognized because you give them your undivided attention. In truth, a listening ear can promote more healing than a multitude of words rightly spoken. Besides, God created us with two ears and one mouth, which proves He meant us to listen twice as much as we speak!

GOOD VIBRATIONS

Some Big-Hearted People use music to influence others positively since it can promote peace, tranquility, and healing. Music can often go where words cannot. Do you play a musical instrument? Volunteer to play for people every opportunity you can. It doesn't matter if it's for one person or one thousand people. Just bring your instrument (maybe your voice is your instrument) and let your gift of music be something special to those who hear it. I have seen the effects of playing an instrument to a small group of people in an intimate setting. The results are remarkable.

A good friend and professional therapeutic harpist, Dr. Diane Schneider, shared this with me:

> Since mothers began singing to babies to soothe their colic and quiet them to sleep, we have experienced the healing power of music. From biblical times, the best-known example of healing with music is the story of David playing his harp to heal King Saul. Gradually, over many centuries of careful observation in numerous cultures, a body of belief and practice emerged. Specifically, it involved the use of music vibrations to treat certain conditions such as anxiety, sleeplessness, pain, and depression. I have personally seen God perform miraculous physical healings—including from coma states—and great peace of mind and spirit happen to patients and their families through music. (For a more detailed description of music therapy, see the Appendix.)

BEHIND THE SCENES

Occasionally my wife and I enjoy attending plays or popular musicals. More often than not, we're astounded at the quality and beauty of the performance. Sometimes we're amazed at the range and clarity of the singer's voices or we sit spellbound as the actors portray their roles with unparalleled skill. In typical fashion, the actors, singers, and orchestra conductors come out at the end of the performance to receive applause from the audience. To think that only those performing onstage were responsible for a successful presentation would be presumptuous.

Behind the scenes you would find stage-hands, sound and lighting technicians, costume specialists, choreographers, and a host of others providing support. Usually the only acknowledgment given to these talented people is in the credits listed in the program guide. Yet without their participation and expertise the show would be less than stimulating—and more likely, the performance wouldn't even take place.

> Music can often go where words cannot.

Therefore it's obvious that if those working behind the scenes are absent, the endeavor will be mediocre or fail altogether. Maybe you have a gift where you perform your work behind the scenes but it often goes unnoticed. Take heart; God's Word declares that your acts of Big-Heartedness, no matter how small, will glorify Him.

> Be quick to give a meal to the hungry, a bed to the homeless—cheerfully. Be generous with the different things God gave you, passing them around so all get in on it: if words, let it be God's words; if help, let it be God's hearty help. That way, God's bright presence will be evident in everything through Jesus, and he'll get all the credit as the One mighty in everything—encores to the end of time. Oh, yes!
>
> —1 PETER 4:9–11, THE MESSAGE

12

SIMPLY ORDINARY

Perfection consists not in doing extraordinary things, but in doing ordinary things extraordinary well. Neglect nothing; the most trivial action may be performed to God.

—ANGÉLIQUE ARNAULD[1]

ORDINARY PEOPLE

"God uses ordinary people." It's a simple and straightforward phrase needing no explanation. You can find it in music, poems, and in many books. Like me, you have probably heard or read these four words many times. But do you believe it deep-down inside, particularly if it refers to you? Throughout the pages of the Bible, we find plain, ordinary men and women whom God used to carry out His will. These outstanding historic accounts of "extraordinary ordinaries" give us inspiration and encouragement. Yet, sometimes we find it difficult to believe that God would perform His great purposes similarly through us. We often view others whom God uses in a special way as being supremely favored. This simply isn't true. God does not respect one person more than another. (See Acts 10:34.) If we look closely at their lives, it's obvious they were simply ordinary—just like us. One such person was Gideon.

GOD'S MIGHTY WARRIOR

Before the reign of kings in Israel, God raised up judges to lead His people. During this four hundred–year span in Israel's timeline, the children of Israel often wandered from God and did evil by serving pagan gods. Because of this idolatry, God allowed their enemies—in this case the Midianites—to oppress them. Eventually, the Israelites would cry out to the Lord for help. In His love and mercy, He always answered their desperate plea.

The man Gideon, son of Joash, was threshing wheat in a winepress. Not the usual place to thresh, but he did it secretly, fearing his enemies might see him. Without warning, an angel appeared and spoke with resolve, "The Lord is with you, mighty warrior." Notice the angel did not speak to Gideon as he seemed—an ordinary, fearful man—but what Gideon would be, God's mighty warrior. Now, form this picture in your mind. As Gideon heard these words, he turned right, then left, and glanced behind to see if the angel was talking to someone else. He pivoted about-face and replied, "Who, me? I think you've got the wrong guy. If the Lord's with us, then why are we squirming under Midian's thumb?"

The Lord didn't answer Gideon's question directly. This time He spoke point blank, "Go in the strength you have and save Israel. Aren't I the one sending you?" God was plainly telling him, "Just go as you are with what you have. I'll take care of the rest." Gideon looked at his simple, ordinary self and then answered, "How and with what could I ever save Israel? My clan is the weakest, and I'm the runt of the litter." The Lord trumped Gideon's reply again: "I will be with you, and you will strike down the Midianites."

> Sometimes we tend to look at our lot in life or view our abilities as barely adequate. God sees us quite differently.

Do you see what God was trying to get across to Gideon? Not to look at himself or his lack of stature or ability—but to God, who would be victorious through him. Gideon only saw the raw material, but God saw the end product. This serves as a word of encouragement to us all. Sometimes we tend to look at our lot in life or view our abilities as barely adequate. God sees us quite differently. He looks at what we'll become if we allow Him to perform His will through us. God wants our perspective to agree with His and wants us to realize that He will supply what we need to accomplish the task before us.

Gideon gazed at the hordes of enemies camped in the Valley of Jezreel. As he did, God empowered him with His Spirit. Although God's words encouraged Gideon, he still wasn't up to the task. He had a gnawing impression that he was on God's fast track to warriorhood—but still needed more proof. The wheels of Gideon's thought process turned in his head. "I'll make a sacrificial offering. Yes, great plan." So off he went to give legs to his idea. He could have used other means, but why sacrifice? It's an easy explanation.

Human nature always tries to make itself acceptable to God by its own works, often by doing good deeds or performing some ritual offering. Gideon was no exception. After all, God called him for a great mission, so he had better make sure he was worthy—but God had other ideas. He proved His ownership by coaching Gideon in Sacrifice 101. Here's the fundamental principle: do it God's way. Gideon placed the sacrifice on the altar, and the angel touched it with the tip of his staff. Suddenly, fire flared from the rock and consumed the offering. The shock and awe overwhelmed him, but the Lord encouraged Gideon, saying, "Peace, don't be afraid; you won't die." With his newfound humility, Gideon worshiped God by building an altar.

Let's fast-forward to the next scene. The enemies of Israel, thick as locusts, joined forces and camped against them in the Valley of Jezreel. Immediately, the Scripture declares, "The Spirit of the LORD came upon Gideon and he summoned the armies of Israel." Despite this, Gideon was still not convinced that he was hearing from God. He allowed his thinking to get in the way again and got the pre-battle jitters. He asked God, "If you will save Israel by my hand as promised, confirm it by this sign." His choice was to use a fleece (you have to admit, he was creative). Some still point to this as means to justify using a "fleece" to receive confirmation of God's will.

I believe God patiently complied with Gideon's request to see confirming signs for a reason. Gideon didn't have God's written Word and promises to stand on—but we do. He also wasn't indwelt by the Holy Spirit—but we are. God confirms His will to us mainly by His Word and His Spirit. God's Word illumines our understanding. It enables us to discern His will and live accordingly. The psalmist wrote, "The entrance and unfolding of Your words give light; their unfolding gives understanding (discernment and comprehension) to the simple" (Ps. 119:130, AMP). As highlighted in chapter 7 (and as will be revisited in chapter 16), we learn to hear the Holy Spirit by spending time with Him in the secret place, by getting quiet and listening.

However, sometimes He will use a third component, members of Christ's body. Through frequent fellowship, members of His body confirm God's Word to us.

> We do not use words of man's wisdom. We use words given to us by the Holy Spirit. We use these words to tell what the Holy Spirit wants to say to those who put their trust in Him.
> —1 CORINTHIANS 2:13, NEW LIFE

In this case there must be agreement between all three—God's Word, His Spirit, and Christ's body.

The ever-patient Lord responded to Gideon's request twice and confirmed

His will by means of the fleece. The Gideon-ordinary then became the Spirit-empowered extraordinary and was ready to lead in battle—this time without a doubt. The next morning God's warrior and thirty-two thousand men were decked out in battle array. However, the Lord placed a lock hold on their war plan. He told Gideon, "I know you psyched yourself for war, but you have too many men. Tell those trembling with fear to leave." The staccato sound of twenty-two thousand hurried footsteps echoed in the camp. When the dust settled, ten thousand remained. Gideon swallowed hard, but before speaking he heard the Lord again. "There are still too many men." He broke into a sweat, but God showed him how to sift the open-eyed vigilant from the carefree half-hearted. The ranks dwindled to three hundred warriors, and Gideon sent the rest packing.

Gideon then realized what God had previously tried to show him. The only way a few hundred could defeat many thousands was through God—not in the might or power of man but by God's spirit alone. The Lord revealed to Gideon that He would deliver the entire enemy camp into his hand.

The Spirit adrenaline pulsed through Gideon, who divided his men into three companies. He placed trumpets and empty jars in their hands with torches inside. They went to the edge of the enemy's camp, and there Gideon spoke softly. "Watch me and follow my lead. Do exactly as I do. When I and all who are with me blow our trumpets, then from all around the camp blow yours and shout, 'The sword of the Lord and of Gideon.'" Each man held his position and on Gideon's signal blew the trumpets, smashed the jars, and shouted. The enemy cried out in panic, while the Lord caused them to turn their swords on each other. Gideon called out men from the tribes of Israel to aid in the pursuit. They destroyed those fleeing on foot. The Israelites subdued their enemies, and during Gideon's lifetime, they enjoyed forty years of peace. (See Judges chapters 6 and 7.)

Therefore, as with Gideon, our formula for victory is the same:

Simply ordinary person + God = Victory

God may never ask us to do something for Him and others as dramatic as what Gideon did. However, no matter what God calls us to do, large or small, He will surely use us—just as we are and where we are.

Those in the early church were simply ordinary folk, too. Paul affirmed this in His letter to the church in Corinth—a real bunch of characters.

Take a good look, friends, at who you were when you got called into this life. I don't see many of "the brightest and the best" among you, not many influential, not many from high-society families. Isn't it obvious that God deliberately chose men and women that the culture overlooks and exploits and abuses, chose these "nobodies" to expose the hollow pretensions of the "somebodies"? That makes it quite clear that none of you can get by with blowing your own horn before God. Everything that we have—right thinking and right living, a clean slate and a fresh start—comes from God by way of Jesus Christ. That is why we have the saying, "If you're going to blow a horn, blow a trumpet for God."

—1 Corinthians 1:26–29, The Message

Verses like this help us to realize we can glorify God and bless others, regardless of our background or qualifications.

"Ordinary" Gifts

Some people share a common view that sounds something like this: "I can accept that God uses ordinary people; but my gifts are ordinary, too. I just wish I could see greater results." In answer to this, let me rephrase this chapter's opening quotation: "God uses ordinary people with ordinary gifts." That's right. When you use your gifts, no matter how simple, the results will be great—exactly as God intended. Who decides the value of the fruit you produce? It's not you or anyone else; God is the one who gives the increase. Paul described this using an example we can easily understand: "I planted the seed. Apollos watered it, but it was God Who kept it growing. This shows the one who plants or the one who waters is not the important one. God is the important One. He makes it grow. The one who plants and the one who waters are alike. Each one will receive his own reward" (1 Cor. 3:6–8, New Life).

> However, no matter what God calls us to do, large or small, He will surely use us—just as we are and where we are.

Paul reminds us that God gives a diversity of gifts to the body of Christ. He outlined this by sketching a word picture using the human body as his model.

You can easily enough see how this kind of thing works by looking no further than your own body. Your body has many parts—limbs, organs, cells—but no matter how many parts you can name, you're still one body.... A body isn't just a single part blown up into something huge. It's all the different—but—similar parts arranged and functioning together. If Foot said, "I'm not elegant like Hand, embellished with rings; I guess I don't belong to this body," would that make it so? If Ear said, "I'm not beautiful like Eye, limpid and expressive; I don't deserve a place on the head," would you want to remove it from the body? If the body was all eye, how could it hear? If all ear, how could it smell? As it is, we see that God has carefully placed each part of the body right where he wanted it.... What we have is one body with many parts, each its proper size and in its proper place. No part is important on its own.

—1 CORINTHIANS 12:12–20, THE MESSAGE

Therefore, it doesn't matter how ordinary we may view our gifts; not one is any less or more important than anyone else's. There may be people with abilities that place them in the spotlight. Some view them as talented and fruitful. However, if we focus on the person's abilities alone, we develop a lopsided view. We might even imagine that if we had someone else's gift we would be happier. To think so would infer that God made a mistake when He created us. In all honesty, another's gift would not make us happy. We would be downright miserable, because that's not what God intended for us.

> Therefore, it doesn't matter how ordinary we may view our gifts; not one is any less or more important than anyone else's.

God will never help us to become someone that we're not. Besides, would we want the responsibility that comes with it? Jesus spoke plainly when He told us, "From everyone who has been given much, much will be demanded; and from the one who has been entrusted with much, much more will be asked" (Luke 12:48, NIV). God knows what we can handle and would not give us anything that would overwhelm us. He created each of us in perfection with the most suitable gifts we need to glorify Him.

Psalm 139 beautifully depicts how God formed us and followed our growth from the time of conception.

Oh, yes, you shaped me first inside, then out; you formed me in my mother's womb. I thank you, High God—you're breathtaking! Body and soul, I am marvelously made! I worship in adoration— what a creation! You know me inside and out, you know every bone in my body; You know exactly how I was made, bit by bit, how I was sculpted from nothing into something. Like an open book, you watched me grow from conception to birth; all the stages of my life were spread out before you, The days of my life all prepared before I'd even lived one day.

—PSALM 139:13–16, THE MESSAGE

God uniquely knit together our entire composition—spirit, soul, and body—and from God's perspective, it's perfect. Do you agree with that statement? If we view ourselves any less than the way God does, we need to change the way we think. Once our thought patterns line up with His, we can effectively use our gifts to bless others and do it with joy.

Before God created the heavens and Earth, He already conceived the role you would play in His great plan of redemption. The way we express our gifts plays a necessary and important part of something larger, more wonderful, and farther-reaching than we can imagine. Each simple act of Big-Heartedness becomes an essential part of the sum total of God's great plan. We are His Big-Hearted representatives in this world and can shape the future of people's lives for good—eternally!

13

THE STRENGTH OF ENCOURAGEMENT

Keep encouraging and edifying one another,
just as you have been doing.

—1 Thessalonians 5:11, author's paraphrase

After completing my formal education in 1971, I worked at a machine tool company in the drafting and design department. My usual lunchtime custom was to study the Bible. One day while reading the Book of Isaiah, a particular scripture leapt out at me. I sensed the Holy Spirit impress on my spirit that the verse was a word of encouragement for the pastor of my church. So immediately, I picked up the phone and dialed the church office. When I asked to speak to him, the secretary told me he was unavailable but agreed to take a message. I shared the Scripture reference with her and asked her to give it to the pastor as soon as possible. No doubt, my voice revealed the urgency, because she did exactly as I asked when she saw him. However, at the time he was busy, so He folded the note and placed it in his pocket to read later.

This is his account of the events that transpired during the next few hours:

> I attended a Bible study in the evening and a young man approached me with his Bible. He shared a verse with me that stood out to him earlier in the day. He sensed it was specifically for me. I read the scripture and as I did, remembered the secretary gave me a note earlier in the day. As I unfolded the creased paper, I noticed that it was the same verse the young man just handed to me. I became both elated and humbled as I read these words since it was a day when I desperately needed encouragement.

"For the mountains shall depart And the hills be removed, But My kindness shall not depart from you, Nor shall My covenant of peace be removed," Says the LORD, who has mercy on you.

—ISAIAH 54:10, NKJV

Neither I nor my friend had any foreknowledge the pastor needed encouragement on that particular day. Two people simply responded in obedience to God, which caused someone to receive an affirmation of His kindness and mercy. Some people would dismiss this as merely a coincidence. Personally, I don't believe there are any coincidences in the life of a Christian. Everything happens for a specific reason, though we may not always understand why. Be assured, the same God who knows the number of hairs on our heads orchestrates our lives and events to coincide with His divine purpose. As mentioned earlier, everything we do to bless others, whether small or large, plays an important part in God's intricately designed plan. The take-away from this is to understand how important it is to rely on the Holy Spirit in our daily activities.

> Be assured, the same God who knows the number of hairs on our heads orchestrates our lives and events to coincide with His divine purpose.

THE POWER OF WORDS

In the first chapter of Genesis we read that God said, "Let there be light," and there was light (v. 3, NIV). God created the heavens, Earth, and all that is in them by His spoken Word. His creative words brought forth life. When He finished, He pronounced it all good. The Bible also declares that Jesus upholds all things by the word of His power. (See Hebrews 1:3.) Our words have power to be creative as well. They have the power to build up and promote healing but also to tear down or destroy. Proverbs 18:21 states, "Words kill, words give life; they're either poison or fruit—you choose" (THE MESSAGE). Another translation puts it this way: "Death and life are in the power of the tongue, and those who love it will eat its fruit" (NKJV).

In our relationships with others, our words can either wound or heal. They are like seeds sown into people's lives. If our words are kind and loving, they will reap a harvest of the same. However, if we sow critical, mean, and spiteful words, they will reap a whirlwind of disaster. I meet so many people who live in defeat because they believe what someone said to them when they were young.

"It's all your fault."

"You're just mediocre."

"You're nothing but a loser."

"You'll never amount to anything."

These negative words held people captive; but in reality, they were nothing but lies!

On the other hand, there are people who did well and became successful because their parents, a teacher, a coach, a youth pastor, or a grandparent spoke words of encouragement and blessing to them.

"I know you can do it."

"You are greatly loved."

"You've got what it takes."

"With God, you can accomplish anything."

Jesus told us, "For out of the abundance of the heart the mouth speaks. A good man out of the good treasure of his heart brings forth good things, and an evil man out of the evil treasure brings forth evil things" (Matt. 12:34–35, NKJV). This is because He knows that whatever we think about, meditate on, read, or look upon will affect what comes out of our mouth. Simply stated, what the mind conceives, the mouth speaks. Therefore, we should be careful what we feed our soul and spirit. The Book of Proverbs places a strong emphasis on this by using words like *guard* and *vigilance*. Proverbs 4:23 states, "Keep and guard your heart with all vigilance and above all that you guard, for out of it flow the springs [or fountains] of life" (AMP). Not only does God want us to think with our minds but also to mind what we think.

So, what should occupy our thoughts? The Book of Philippians provides the answer: "Finally, brothers, whatever is true, whatever is noble, whatever is right, whatever is pure, whatever is lovely, whatever is admirable—if anything is excellent or praiseworthy—think about such things" (Phil. 4:8, NIV).

I've noticed that if I spend too much time watching, reading, or listening to the world news reports, it affects my spirit. I can easily become fearful, critical, or angry, and it affects my conversation. I find that I must change my mind's focus if I want a better thought life and to have my words positively influence others. I must also make a conscious effort by choosing to speak uplifting words often. I have also discovered that as I daily fellowship with God and take in His Word, I'm more likely to speak with kindness and encouragement.

WHERE SELDOM IS HEARD AN *ENCOURAGING* WORD?

The place where we can accurately evaluate our words is in relationships with family members. The way we speak and act at home reveals who we are—not at work, not in church, not in public, but at home. Since we live in such close proximity within our families, we often say things in unguarded moments that reveal the true state of our hearts. And when someone offends or hurts us, what comes out of our mouth sometimes just ain't pretty. Family members have become wounded and entire families devastated by words hastily spoken in anger. Sometimes it takes years to recover, and usually a recovery only occurs because someone asked for forgiveness in humility.

In retrospect, the words I regret the most are ones that I've spoken to those nearest and dearest to me. I wish I could somehow go back in time, relive the moment, and change my words. However, once I spoke, the words were irretrievable.

> The way we speak and act at home reveals who we are—not at work, not in church, not in public, but at home.

The apostle James shows us how to appraise our spiritual life by listening to the words we speak. He wrote, "If anyone considers himself religious and yet does not keep a tight rein on his tongue, he deceives himself and his religion is worthless" (James 1:26, NIV). *Worthless*—that's a strong word, but there's no getting around it. This simply stresses the degree of importance that God places on the words we speak.

In James 3, he continues to expound on what he referred to as the unruly (wild and undisciplined) member of our body, the tongue.

> For we all stumble in many things. If anyone does not stumble in word, he is a perfect man, able also to bridle the whole body.
>
> —JAMES 3:2, NKJV

Simple interpretation—if we can control our tongues, any other form of self-discipline is a piece of cake.

In chapter 6, I discussed the need to evaluate our love walk. Well, it's just as important to assess our love talk too. There is no better place to practice love talk and encouragement than at home. And when I use the word *practice*, that's exactly what I mean. For most of us, love talk doesn't come naturally (especially for us guys), so we need to make a resolute decision to speak graciously with words of love and encouragement. And as we do, we'll begin to experience harmony and peace instead of discord and strife.

What about speaking words of appreciation? It doesn't take much to speak words like this:

- "That was a great dinner, honey! I appreciate your hard work and the time you took to prepare this meal."
- "Thanks for taking me shopping, Mom. I appreciate you buying these new clothes for me."
- "Dear, I appreciate the time you spent with me and the children tonight, especially after you worked a long day."
- "I am so proud of you for studying hard to get good grades. I appreciate your dedication."

ENCOURAGING YOURSELF

Occasionally, we are the ones who need encouragement. The Lord may send someone to inspire and encourage us. He may place something in our way for us to read or hear that may hearten us as well. Yet sometimes external sources of encouragement are absent. So when we're going through a difficult time or when everything seems hopeless, what should we do? An experience of David, king of Israel, answers this question.

In 1 Samuel 30, we read that David and his men of war traveled to the city of Ziklag. The anticipated joy of uniting with their families quickly faded. In the distance, they saw clouds of smoke billowing from the city. Upon arriving, only the acrid air and scenes of destruction greeted them. The Amalekites sacked and burnt Ziklag and took the women and children captive. The anger of David's men kindled against him. He was definitely not having a good day.

> And David was greatly distressed; for the people spake of stoning him, because the soul of all the people was grieved, every man for his sons and for his daughters: but David encouraged himself in the LORD his God.
>
> —1 SAMUEL 30:6, KJV

Later in Samuel's account, David asked the Lord for His direction and received it. He then advanced to rout the enemy and recovered everything the Amalekites had taken. However, it is the last part of this verse that contains an unexpected phrase—one that reveals the true heart of David: "David encouraged himself in the LORD his God."

When everything looked bleak, David refused to consider the dire circumstances and the angry faces of his men. He intently focused on the Lord. David encouraged himself by remembering how God delivered him in the past. We see plentiful evidence of this in the psalms, such as Psalm 63:6–7: "When I remember You upon my bed and meditate on You in the night watches. For You have been my help, and in the shadow of Your wings will I rejoice" (AMP).

Even as a youth, he remembered his former victories, especially the time he watched the boasting windbag Goliath of Gath mocking the armies of Israel. King Saul did his best to discourage David from fighting the giant. He compared David's youthful inexperience to Goliath's superior warrior skills, but David didn't flinch. He declared to Saul that he would slay Goliath just like he killed the lion and bear that attacked his sheep.

The Bible tells us David picked up five smooth stones to use in his sling. Why would David need five? Some falsely claim that it was just in case David's first stone didn't hit its target. But when you research the account in the Book of 2 Samuel, you discover that Goliath had four giant brothers. And just in case, David had a stone to take out each one!

Next, we see David speak in faith by boldly proclaiming victory to the giant's face: "This day the LORD will hand you over to me, and I'll strike you down and cut off your head. Today I will give the carcasses of the Philistine army to the birds of the air and the beasts of the earth, and the whole world will know that there is a God in Israel. All those gathered here will know that it is not by sword or spear that the LORD saves; for the battle is the LORD's, and he will give all of you into our hands" (1 Sam. 17:46–47, NIV). He then ran toward Goliath, swung his sling, and embedded a stone in Goliath's forehead.

Now let me ask you a question. Do you think a young man would have enough strength to kill a giant—who was over nine feet tall—by striking him with a stone? In the natural realm, I don't. However, it was not David's stone that slew Goliath but God's supernatural power behind the stone! No doubt David realized that God had to come through or he was history. But since he knew the battle was the Lord's, he stepped out in faith and God gave the victory to David and Israel.

This highlights a simple solution you can use to overcome your personal Goliaths, but you must make a choice. If you focus on the giants you lose, but if you focus on the God of victory you win. You can choose to look at the circumstances or choose to look at God's Word.

A valuable lesson unfolds as we break down David's experience further.

- He remembered.
- He meditated.
- He spoke words of faith.

REMEMBERING

Many refer to the Old Testament prophet Jeremiah as the weeping prophet. Read about his life and the condition of God's people Israel during that time in history. Once you do, I'm certain you'll agree that this alias suited him well. His love affair with depression is painfully obvious in the third chapter of Lamentations. Listening to his words, you would think that God hated him; it seems Jeremiah thought so, too. He wrote things like, "I have known God's

> If you focus on the giants you lose, but if you focus on the God of victory you win.

anger....felt the back of His hand....I am a target for His arrows....He locks up my cries and groans and tosses the key....I'm a goner....a lost cause." But this is only a sampling of the weeping prophet's diatribe. Yet God wasn't wringing His hands wishing He chose another prophet to declare His Word.

In modern language, we would say, "God just let him spew his guts." Some would call him a blasphemer; that is, until they read further. The Holy Spirit simply touched Jeremiah's heartstrings. His memory rebounded with energy, and he spoke words of a different sort: "But there's one other thing I remember, and remembering, I keep a grip on hope: God's loyal love couldn't have run out, his merciful love couldn't have dried up. They're created new every morning. How great your faithfulness! I'm sticking with God (I say it over and over). He's all I've got left" (Lam. 3:21–24, THE MESSAGE).

That's exactly how we encourage ourselves. We remember when God showed Himself strong on our behalf, those times when He met our deepest needs. You might bring to mind testimonies of friends or family members who experienced God's provision in a supernatural way. Write down your victories in a journal. Those times where God came through and:

- He miraculously healed your child.
- He delivered you from serious injury.
- He provided money to meet a desperate family need.
- He comforted you after the death of a loved one.

Steadfastly refuse circumstances to move you and allow the Holy Spirit to bring these past victories to your mind. The undergirding of your faith occurs when you continue to build on every victory, no matter how small.

MEDITATING

Sometimes the word *meditation* flashes a wrong image to some people. They usually think of Eastern mysticism—someone sitting in the lotus position repeating some secret mantra. But meditating simply means to reflect on, ponder, or to continually go over something in your mind. A descriptive example—you'll most likely not forget this one—is a cow chewing (or ruminating) its cud. The cow chews and swallows food to digest it partially. Brought up again as a cud (a softened food ball), the cow re-chews, and repeats the process until it's fully digested. I think you get the point from this rather earthy example.

Who and what should be the source of our meditation? God and the promises in His Word. We see this verified throughout the Bible and especially in the psalms.

- I *meditate* on your Word.
- I *meditate* on your wonders.
- I *meditate* on your promises.
- I *meditate* on your unfailing love.
- I *meditate* on your wonderful works.

As we continually meditate on God's Word, it goes deep down into our spirits. Head knowledge becomes heart knowledge. His Word is living and powerful.

> For the word of God is living and active. Sharper than any double-edged sword, it penetrates even to dividing soul and spirit, joints and marrow; it judges the thoughts and attitudes of the heart.
> —HEBREWS 4:12, NIV

SPEAKING WORDS OF FAITH

As mentioned earlier, our words are a creative force; they have power for life or death, to heal or wound. However, when we speak God's Word, it always brings life, healing, hope, and encouragement.

Since the power of God is resident in His living Word, we activate that same power when we speak it. Come before the Lord and remind Him of His Word. Say, "Father this is what your word says, and I believe your promises. I call these things that do not exist as though they did." (See Romans 4:17.)

When thoughts of fear torment you, respond, "God has not given me the spirit of fear [or timidity]; but of power, love and a sound mind" (2 Tim. 1:7, author's paraphrase.)

If the task before you seems insurmountable, proclaim, "I can do all things through Christ who strengthens me" (Phil. 4:13, NKJV).

If the temptation to become discouraged and give up invades your mind, shout, "But You, O LORD, are a covering around me, my shining-greatness, and the One Who lifts my head" (Ps. 3:3, NEW LIFE).

> The undergirding of your faith occurs when you continue to build on every victory, no matter how small.

If a great financial need towers above you like a mountain, declare, "But my God shall supply all my need according to his riches in glory by Christ Jesus" (Phil. 4:19, KJV).

This is not mind over matter, as some would suggest. It is simply confessing that God's Word is true and reliable. Also, by giving voice we confirm His covenant relationship with us.

Purpose each day to look for opportunities to be an encourager. God will bring those into your life who need a positive and uplifting word. Words of blessing and encouragement reflect the manner of Big-Hearted People. They realize the power of their words to strengthen, heal, and bring comfort, but most importantly, to glorify God. May others say about us the same things the apostle Paul said to Philemon: "For I have derived great joy and comfort and encouragement from your love, because the hearts of the saints [who are your fellow Christians] have been cheered and refreshed through you, [my] brother" (Philem. 1:7, AMP).

14

PRAYING FOR DEAR LIFE

Lord, help me live from day to day
In such a self-forgetful way,
That even when I kneel to pray,
My prayer shall be for—others.

—CHARLES DELUCENA MEIGS, *OTHERS*[1]

Prayer is not conquering God's reluctance, but
taking hold of God's willingness.

—PHILLIPS BROOKS[2]

*I*f you were one of Jesus' disciples during His earthly ministry and could ask Him anything, what would it be? Would you request the ability to heal the sick or raise the dead? To preach the gospel to thousands or miraculously feed the hungry?

His disciples were with Him daily, and the Scriptures highlight an occasion in which they asked Jesus to do something special for them. As was His custom, Jesus was spending time in prayer with His Father. His disciples waited until He finished and asked Him, "Lord, teach us to pray" (Luke 11:1, NKJV). Jesus answered their request by teaching them a simple but far-reaching prayer known to us as the Our Father. Jesus recognized the value of prayer. The Bible tells us that He would often spend all night in prayer. Therefore, if He valued it so highly, should we not consider it just as important to us as well? You may ask, How should I pray, and how can prayer make me more effective as a Big-Hearted Person? The answers form the focus of this chapter.

Despite a large variety of books on prayer available today, some people think of prayer as a hit-or-miss game. Their thoughts suggest that sometimes you hit a home run but sometimes you strike out. My use of the word *game* here does have significance. Let me explain.

When we think of games, it probably brings to mind particular sports like baseball, football, basketball, and hockey. If you attend a football game, you would see it played by football rules. If you tried to play football by baseball rules, it wouldn't work (though it would be very amusing). "Sports" may be the category, but you play each sport by its own set of rules.

God does not review some heavenly checklist to ensure that you have prayed correctly.

Similarly, prayer may be the category, but there are several different forms of prayer, a specific reason for each and an expected outcome. Some common prayers are those of petition, dedication, confession, and intercession. In this chapter I will highlight the prayer of intercession in its simplest definition— praying for others. My intent is not to offer you a tried and true formula or "ten easy steps that anyone can use" to pray effectively. God does not review some heavenly checklist to ensure that you have prayed correctly. You will begin to see this more clearly as the truth of God's Word comes alive in this chapter.

I find enjoyment in reading quotations on religious themes and human nature. In leafing through pages and pages of quotations about prayer for this book, my research reminded me of an attitude into which we so easily fall. I'm referring to self-centered prayers of petition. Out of literally hundreds of quotes, I found few that highlight how important it is to pray for others.

The title of this chapter, "Praying for Dear Life," may bring to mind images of someone in dire need, praying in desperation with everything they've got— for dear life. However, that is not my message at all. It is simply this: praying for those who are dear—dear to us, but especially dear to the heart of God. Please realize that it is not wrong or selfish to pray for ourselves. Jesus encouraged us by saying, "For sure, I tell you, My Father will give you whatever you ask in My name. Until now you have not asked for anything in My name. Ask and you will receive. Then your joy will be full" (John 16:23–24, NEW LIFE). We can pray with power, boldness, and confidence that our prayers will produce results.

> This is the confidence we have in approaching God: that if we ask anything according to his will, he hears us. And if we know that he hears us—whatever we ask—we know that we have what we asked of him.
>
> —1 JOHN 5:14–15, NIV

We are all familiar with the saying "Prayer changes things," and through personal experience we know that it's true. Yet, there exists the tendency to wait and pray only when things get desperate or after we have tried to change things by our own efforts—and failed. However, prayer should always be the first thing we do, even in small matters.

> Don't fret or worry. Instead of worrying, pray. Let petitions and praises shape your worries into prayers, letting God know your concerns. Before you know it, a sense of God's wholeness, everything coming together for good, will come and settle you down. It's wonderful what happens when Christ displaces worry at the center of your life.
>
> —Philippians 4:6–7, The Message

Intercession 101

Intercessory prayer is so vast in scope that you can find entire books written on this subject. I could easily expand this chapter to provide an in-depth look and share testimonies about this Spirit-led form of prayer. However, my purpose is not to provide an all-encompassing guide to the prayer of intercession but to help you to see how God uses yielded vessels, even in the simplest ways, to prevail in prayer for others.

The prayer of intercession is selfless because we change our focus from ourselves to others. It is voluntary on our part because God will never force us to pray. As we are willing, the Holy Spirit will lead us in prayer for a person, many people, or maybe a nation. We may pray by ourselves or pray in agreement with others. A verse that is familiar to intercessors is 2 Chronicles 7:14: "If my people, who are called by my name, will humble themselves and pray and seek my face and turn from their wicked ways, then will I hear from heaven and will forgive their sin and will heal their land" (NIV). This verse highlights what God requires for successful intercession—even to the degree of healing an entire nation.

- *Availability*: God looks for people who are willing to pray for others.
- *Responsibility*: One must understand the responsibility of an intercessor and persevere (importune) in prayer until a breakthrough occurs.

- *Humility*: Successful intercession is not possible until we realize it's not us or even the way we pray that brings about healing and restoration, but God alone.
- *Seeking God*: Intercessors spend time with Him, discover His heart in each circumstance, and pray accordingly.
- *Turning from sin*: In repentance, we must be diligent not to allow unconfessed sin to take root in our lives and defile us.

This is the foundation of intercession. Once we resolve to be obedient to God according to His Word, we have assurance that our prayers will be effectual. The apostle John shows agreement by declaring, "Dear friends, if our hearts do not condemn us, we have confidence before God and receive from him anything we ask, because we obey his commands and do what pleases him" (1 John 3:21–22, NIV).

FATHER KNOWS BEST

When we pray, we should guard against thinking that suggests we know the best way for God to answer our prayers for ourselves or others. I have fallen into this trap occasionally. Rarely has God answered my prayers exactly the way I thought He would—and I'm glad. I have discovered that I'd rather leave the results to His sovereign will since *He* knows best. Let me explain.

I dated a young woman in my teen years, but at the time, my life was a real mess. However, a few years later, the Lord changed my life. I thought there might be a chance that she and I could get together again. I began asking God to work things out between us because I thought she would make a good wife. I even reminded Him of all her fine qualities (as if He didn't already know). I spent much time in prayer trying to convince God that she was clearly the best choice. Yet He showed me through certain circumstances that she didn't care for me and was not His choice anyway.

After recovering from my disappointment, I yielded my will to His in the matter. Just a few weeks later, I met the lovely young woman whom I would eventually marry. God brought it about in such a miraculous way that I knew beyond any doubt that she was His choice for me. After thirty-six years of marriage, I still thank God that He didn't answer my first prayer for a wife in the way that I wanted.

EMPATHY BY THE SPIRIT

A word often used to describe the manner in which we intercede is *supplication*, meaning "to ask for earnestly and humbly."[3] Often God allows us to enter the experience of the one(s) we're praying for and sense what they're feeling so we can pray effectively. We are not praying what our mind tells us but by what the Holy Spirit reveals. I call this empathy by the Spirit.

> So too the [Holy] Spirit comes to our aid and bears us up in our weakness; for we do not know what prayer to offer nor how to offer it worthily as we ought, but the Spirit Himself goes to meet our supplication and pleads in our behalf with unspeakable yearnings and groanings too deep for utterance. And He Who searches the hearts of men knows what is in the mind of the [Holy] Spirit [what His intent is], because the Spirit intercedes and pleads [before God] in behalf of the saints according to and in harmony with God's will.
>
> —ROMANS 8:26–27, AMP

Big-Hearted People place their faith in God's Word when they pray on behalf of others. When Big-Hearted People tell someone they will pray for them, they *really* will pray. I've heard many friends and relatives tell me, "I would rather have you pray for me than give me your time or money. Prayer is the most important thing you can do for me." Their declaration echoes the same sentiment of my heart. Sometimes I can actually sense when people are praying for me.

When we pray, we should guard against thinking that suggests we know the best way for God to answer our prayers for ourselves or others.

Maybe you've experienced that too. Praying for others can also prevent tragedies from occurring. Testimonies abound describing occasions when God awakened people in the middle of the night to intercede for someone. Only later did they discover that their prayers prevented a tragic incident. The prayer of intercession can truly make the difference between life and death.

FAMILIES THAT PRAY TOGETHER

I first remember hearing the phrase "the family that prays together stays together" years ago. It sure sounded nice, and I heard many people say it. However, when I look at the state of the family unit today, I think it was no more than a feel-good expression for most people. Now, that doesn't mean it was a false statement; it just shows that few people did it.

Intercession is an essential form of prayer for parents (or grandparents), especially in these turbulent times. A mother and father who pray together in agreement can fortify the foundations of their family. However, prayer shouldn't only be the first line of defense but also should take an offensive posture as well. We shouldn't wait to pray until something bad happens; we should pray to *prevent* something bad from happening. This should come as no surprise, because it's precisely what Jesus meant in the Our Father when He told us to pray, "Deliver us from evil" (or from the evil one, Matt. 6:13, NIV).

We live in a world in which we face opposition from the spiritual powers of darkness.

> This is no afternoon athletic contest that we'll walk away from and forget about in a couple of hours. This is for keeps, a life-or-death fight to the finish against the Devil and all his angels.
> —EPHESIANS 6:12, THE MESSAGE

We must be diligent to come against these forces in prayer through the authority that we have in Jesus Christ—especially for our families. Yet, some may ask, What exactly is praying in agreement? It is simply when two or more believers pray and agree about what God's Word says related to their prayer request. A personal example can help to provide some insight.

When our daughters were teenagers, my wife and I would pray in agreement for their protection. We confessed Scriptures, and this is a sample of our prayer:

> *Lord, we stand on your Word for our daughters. Since they're going out tonight, we thank you that your hedge of protection surrounds them. Your Word says that "you give your angels charge over them to keep them in all their ways and you preserve them from all evil." We confess that nothing formed against them will prosper and they will come home safely. We agree together that this is so and that you are faithful to your Word. Amen. (See Job 1:10; Psalm 91:11; 121:7–8; and Isaiah 54:17.)*

We never stayed up late and worried about them. Since God never slumbers or sleeps, there was no reason for us to lose any. We went to bed with the assurance that He was in control. It is far better to sleep soundly in faith than to stay up and worry in fear.

I recall a time when my wife and I went on a getaway weekend to St. Augustine, Florida. When we returned, our eldest daughter greeted us in tears. She told us that she and her two sisters were in a car accident, and she had been driving. Fortunately, not one of them received even the smallest injury, though the car received extensive damage. This is just one of many testimonies that I could share about the power of agreement with God's Word. He is forever faithful to watch over His Word to perform it. (See Jeremiah 1:12.)

Jesus underscored the power of the prayer of agreement when He said, "Again, I tell you that if two of you on earth agree about anything you ask for, it will be done for you by my Father in heaven. For where two or three come together in my name, there am I with them" (Matt. 18:19–20, NIV). Do you notice that He said, "It *will* be done," not, "There is a good chance it will be done"? I can assure you that when you start to do this, demonic forces will resist you. They know that this form of prayer can shake the gates of hell.

The power of agreement with God's Word is also found throughout the Bible in just one word—*amen*. Transcribed directly from Old Testament Hebrew to New Testament Greek and into many other languages, it is universal. When said by God, He is declaring, "It is and shall be so." When we say amen, in effect we declare, "So let it be," or, "May it be fulfilled in agreement with His Word." This is the same word used by Jesus in the Gospels when He says, "Verily," or, "I tell you the truth."

> A mother and father who pray together in agreement can fortify the foundations of their family.

Thayer's Lexicon explains the historical significance of the word *amen*: "It was a custom, which passed over from the synagogues to the Christian assemblies, that when he who had read or discoursed, had offered up solemn prayer to God, the others responded Amen, and thus made the substance of what was uttered their own."[4]

I especially like the last part of this quote, because when we say amen, we are essentially making God's Word our own. This makes perfect sense when you read Hebrews 11:1: "Now faith is the substance of things hoped for, the evidence of things not seen" (NJKV). Try this when you pray: end your prayers with "so let it be" or "may it be fulfilled as spoken" instead of "amen"—and believe what you say. As you do, you'll become aware of the power that exists when you agree with God's Word. You'll experience answered prayer and develop a new appreciation for this simple but powerful word.

Husbands, take the spiritual lead in your home and pray with your wife. If you're a single parent, find another single parent or prayer partner and pray together. Be steadfast and you'll see blessings overtake your family. You'll experience a hedge of protection over your children and will have your needs met. When my wife and I interceded for our children, we experienced blessings; when we didn't, there were heartaches. I have seen both sides, so I passionately encourage you to agree together in intercessory prayer for your family.

PRAY WITHOUT CEASING?

Paul encouraged the church in Thessalonica to "pray without ceasing" (1 Thess. 5:17, KJV). You may ask, "How can I pray continually when I'm involved in so many activities each day? I can't expect to be a good employee, student, or parent if I constantly spend time in prayer." Certainly, this is a legitimate question when we consider Paul's exhortation. As I mentioned previously, the Bible describes specific forms of prayer, and there are certain ways to pray. By saying, "Pray without ceasing," Paul was telling us to keep an *attitude* of prayer in the heart always. Even though we may be busy and our thoughts occupied with daily responsibilities, our spirits can still commune with God.

> Husbands, take the spiritual lead in your home and pray with your wife.

Prayer is like spiritual breathing. Our natural life functions normally when sustained by breathing. The same is true with our spiritual life. Acts 17:28 tells us that "in Him [God] we live and move and have our being" (KJV). Since this describes the intertwining of our life with His, then through prayer, we commune with the Holy Spirit, who sustains us spiritually. Prayer also strengthens our intimate fellowship with Jesus and allows His power to flow through us to others.

I've tried to be sensitive to the Holy Spirit each day during thirty-eight years of employment at different companies. Literally hundreds of times I have passed someone in the hallway, seen someone at their desk, or even noticed a particular person in a meeting and have prayed for them. I may or may not have known them or their needs. Yet, I allow the Holy Spirit to reveal how I should pray for them at that moment. Occasionally I received confirmation about why I was praying for someone, either through conversations or just by asking. However, for the majority of cases, I'm content to wait until eternity, where God will reveal it to me. At times, someone suddenly comes to my mind. I try not to dismiss the thought but pray for that person as the Holy Spirit leads me. I often discover the person I'm praying for has an urgent need for prayer at that moment. Many of my friends and relatives share this same experience. Maybe this happens to you as well.

Prevailing prayer can produce astounding results. James 5:16 tells us, "Therefore confess your sins to one another and pray for one another that you may be healed. The prayer of a righteous man (or women) is filled with dynamic power and very effective" (author's paraphrase). Here we see that our prayers can be powerful and effective since we are righteous through the blood of Jesus Christ. But why does James preface the reference to prayer with "confess your sins to each other"? I'm glad you asked! Let's take a closer look.

SPIRITUALLY CONNECTING

A wonderful healing takes place when we open our hearts to fellow believers. It also establishes a spiritual connection that strengthens the power of agreement. Please allow me to give an example of what I mean and at the same time offer a word of caution.

Several years ago, I requested prayer from a good friend. I was struggling with fleshly desires that I knew weren't pleasing to the Lord and hindered my walk with Him. As I described these conflicts, my friend spoke up and said, "You are struggling with that?" I quickly replied, "Who do you think I am? Someone that doesn't have to fight inner battles like other Christians?" He expressed his willingness to pray for me. I also sensed his relief. His overinflated opinion of me melted into the realization that he wasn't alone in his struggles against sin. That brief exchange helped us center our spirits together in Christ and reinforced our ability to pray effectually.

The early church needed reminding of this, too. Peter wrote to fellow Christians, "Be self-controlled and alert. Your enemy the devil prowls around like a roaring lion looking for someone to devour. Resist him, standing firm in the faith, because you know that your brothers throughout the world are undergoing the same kind of sufferings" (1 Pet. 5:8–9, NIV). Also, Paul wrote to the church in Galatia, "Live creatively, friends. If someone falls into sin, forgivingly restore him, saving your critical comments for yourself. You might be needing forgiveness before the day's out. Stoop down and reach out to those who are oppressed. Share their burdens, and so complete Christ's law. If you think you are too good for that, you are badly deceived" (Gal. 6:1–3, THE MESSAGE). Again, we see a reference to the importance of forgiveness, which I highlighted in chapter 8.

Before continuing, I must issue this warning: be careful to whom you share your faults or personal struggles. Pray and ask the Holy Spirit to lead you to the right person. When you reveal your inner heart to someone, you become

> Even though we may be busy and our thoughts occupied with daily responsibilities, our spirits can still commune with God.

vulnerable and expose your soul. Not everyone who follows Christ is at the same spiritual level. Some Christians are young in the faith and immature. In contrast, others have an intimate love walk with the Lord and are trustworthy. I know someone who shared some personal secrets with a so-called friend. This person betrayed her trust and shared it with someone else. The result of that indiscretion was a bitter divorce and a deeply wounded family. Please ensure the one in whom you confide is a solid, mature Christian who is "walking the walk," not just "talking the talk."

FAITH STEALERS

Some people ask God for too little instead of asking for too much. They think He somehow limits what He will do for them (or for others). The only things that limit God's blessings are fear and its companion, doubt. Remember, fear operates in Satan's realm; faith operates in God's realm. Think about that carefully. Throughout the Gospels, Jesus told His disciples and the common people, "Fear not," or, "Do not be afraid." He knew the paralyzing effects of fear. He knew that fear and doubt are faith-stealers. So how can we discover an effective way to intercede for others? First, by realizing that the cornerstone of effectual prayer is faith.

> And without faith it is impossible to please God, because anyone who comes to him must believe that he exists and that he rewards those who earnestly seek him.
>
> —HEBREWS 11:6, NIV

Second, by understanding that fear and doubt will make our prayers ineffective. Yes, you read it correctly—ineffective. Fear produces weakness; faith produces power. The choice is always the same: believe and receive, or doubt and do without.

Chapter 5 of Mark's Gospel presents a story that contrasts fear and doubt with strong faith. Here we see Jairus, a ruler of the synagogue, earnestly pleading for Jesus to heal his dying child: "My little daughter is dying. Come and lay Your hands on her, so she will be healed and live." Please notice, the faith in Jairus's heart came out of his mouth by saying, "So she will be healed and live." He knew Jesus had authority over sickness and disease and that his daughter would receive healing simply by His touch.

Jesus went with him, but as He got closer to Jairus's home, a group of bad news messengers approached him, saying, "Your daughter is dead, why bother the teacher anymore?" Whoever those people were, they didn't have the same faith as Jairus. They recognized Jesus as only a teacher, but Jairus honored Him as Lord. They insinuated that Jairus bothered or troubled Jesus. Jairus was just asking for something that he knew Jesus would *gladly* do for his daughter.

The Bible states that *immediately* on hearing these words of fear and doubt, Jesus told Jairus, "Do not be afraid, only believe." He knew these negative words were faith stealers. Jesus had to combat the fear and doubt that attacked Jairus's mind by building his faith. This is also how we resist fear and doubt, by exercising our faith through speaking God's Word.

Next we see that Jesus only brought Peter, James, and John with Him as they arrived at Jairus's home. Why didn't He ask the other disciples to come with Him? Though the Scriptures don't explain this, it's very likely that it was because those three believed more than the others did. They might have been earthy and outspoken, but they believed Jesus—and that's what counted. Jesus would not perform miracles to those who were prone to even the smallest doubt. We see that confirmed in Matthew 13:58 as Jesus ministered in His own town. There we read, "And he did not do many miracles there because of their lack of faith" (NIV). Fear and doubt will prevent us from receiving God's blessings as well.

> Remember, fear operates in Satan's realm; faith operates in God's realm.

Once you decide that you're going to believe God's Word, you will come across people who express doubt—it's certain. By their words, you can locate what's in their heart, faith or doubt. They may say, "We're not convinced that God performs miracles today." Rather than base their faith on testimonies of God's faithfulness, they choose to believe negative reports from others. Don't believe what the naysayers speak; believe what God says in His Word.

Arriving at Jairus's house, they witnessed a noisy disturbance and people weeping loudly. Jesus asked them, "What is all this commotion and why are you wailing? The child is not dead but merely sleeping." The people stopped crying and laughed Him to scorn. Again, we see Jesus remove hindrances to faith by putting them outside. Now, only Jesus, His three disciples, Jairus, and his wife were in the room with the little girl. He spoke to her directly, saying, "Little girl, I say unto you arise." She sat up and walked, completely healed. The

Bible says that her parents "were utterly astonished and overcome with amaze-ment" (Mark 5:42, AMP).

As Big-Hearted People, we can see that when we resist the faith stealers of fear and doubt, faith energizes our prayers. And as we intercede with the prayer of faith, it releases God's power to bring forth healing in people's lives.

15

THE GREATEST

A great man stands on God. A small man stands on a great man.

—RALPH WALDO EMERSON[1]

Recently, I was shopping in a store that sells art and noticed something that made me stop and look closely. On the wall hung a large black-and-white, framed photo with the profiles of two celebrated athletes. The complimentary framing and matting enhanced the light and shade elegance of the photograph. However, two words above the photo caught my eye. It simply read, "The Greatest." Now, please hold that thought for a moment and allow me to share two other incidents that caused me to take notice similarly—this time by what I heard.

After I left work one afternoon, I tuned the car radio to a popular talk show just about the time the host introduced his next guest to the audience as "the great one." Another radio show offered an exchange as the host welcomed a caller to the program who responded, "Oh, my God! I'm not worthy; I bow before you."

In all three instances, these laudatory phrases astounded me, yet came as no surprise. No doubt these individuals achieved this status because they excelled in a particular sport or area of endeavor. Yet I believe this confirms a popular trend I have noticed. Much of the global populace seems caught up in a desperate search for heroes, superstars, or even as some suggest—idols. Some celebrities have even gained a cult-like following. People shower them with praise because they obtained a degree of success or notoriety that few achieve. They might exhibit remarkable abilities, great leadership skills, intelligence, exquisite beauty, or perform astounding feats. Even history records its own roll call of "the greats." We easily recognize names like Cyrus the Great, Alexander the Great, Frederick the Great, and Catherine the Great.

In stark contrast, some people's gifts and abilities do not stand out as extraordinary. They are considered less worthy of recognition or public acclamation, and their status is regarded as just average. Yet, those who share these lopsided views are missing the fundamental reason for our existence as human beings, especially our eternal purpose. The primary reason we exist is to glorify God alone, to love and enjoy Him in this life and eternally. Once we establish a personal, vertical relationship with God through Jesus Christ, our supreme goal should be to glorify Him. Second, we allow God, by the person of the Holy Spirit, to work within us to develop our horizontal relationship with others.

> The primary reason we exist is to glorify God alone, to love and enjoy Him in this life and eternally.

Without a secure relationship with God, humanity will always seek to glorify humanity or praise its own works. The apostle Paul confirmed this in his letter to the Romans when he speaks of those who "exchanged the truth of God for a lie and worshiped and served the creature rather than the Creator, Who is blessed forever! Amen (so be it)" (Rom. 1:25, AMP). What some don't understand is that God is the one who gives us all our unique talents and abilities. Our privileged responsibility is to develop them and use them to bless others and glorify Him, not ourselves. As mentioned earlier, publicity or attention does not motivate Big-Hearted People. They don't need to wave a flag to draw attention to them or advertise their generosity. They realize that if they have achieved anything worthy of applause, it is only because of God's enabling and grace.

A STINKING RÉSUMÉ

Regarding stature and accomplishments, Paul of Tarsus was a man who, most would agree, deserved to boast. Look at his credentials, as described in his own words:

> You know my pedigree: a legitimate birth, circumcised on the eighth day; an Israelite from the elite tribe of Benjamin; a strict and devout adherent to God's law; a fiery defender of the purity of my religion, even to the point of persecuting the church; a meticulous observer of everything set down in God's law Book. The very credentials these people are waving around as something special, I'm tearing up and throwing out with the trash—along with everything else I used to take credit for. And why? Because of Christ. Yes, all the things I once thought were so important are gone from my life. Compared to the

high privilege of knowing Christ Jesus as my Master, firsthand, everything I once thought I had going for me is insignificant—dog dung.

—Philippians 3:4–8, The Message

Strong words from one considered well educated and successful.

In the Book of Galatians Paul shared about what he took the most pride in: "May I boast only in this one thing, the cross of our Lord Jesus Christ" (6:14, author's paraphrase). These words bring to mind a hymn that most of us have either sung or heard, "When I Survey the Wondrous Cross" by Isaac Watts. Take a moment, read the first two verses of this hymn, and reflect on the message they convey.

> When I survey the wondrous cross
> On which the Prince of glory died,
> My richest gain I count but loss,
> And pour contempt on all my pride.
>
> Forbid it Lord that I should boast,
> Save in the death of Christ, my God;
> All the vain things that charm me most—
> I sacrifice them to His blood.

The next time we're tempted to boast in our achievements, let's compare them to the cross of Christ, the only true standard. The message in the Old Testament was similar. In this scripture, the Lord God Almighty reveals to His people the only boasting in which He takes delight:

God's message:

"Don't let the wise brag of their wisdom.
Don't let heroes brag of their exploits.
Don't let the rich brag of their riches.
If you brag, brag of this and this only:
That you understand and know me.
I'm God, and I act in loyal love.
I do what's right and set things right and fair,
and delight in those who do the same things.
These are my trademarks." God's decree.

—Jeremiah 9:23–24, The Message

Now before continuing, I wish to clarify my previous statements and bring them into the proper perspective. I'm not saying that we shouldn't set personal life goals. We should enjoy a feeling of accomplishment when we've done well or take pride in our work. And I'm not saying that we shouldn't be proud of our children when they excel or reach the next highest level in their education. The term used to describe this is *authentic pride*, and it's perfectly acceptable. There is nothing wrong with having role models or receiving inspiration by people who overcame obstacles to do great exploits. Some people rightfully deserve recognition. After all, the reason I founded www.bigheartedpeople.com is to provide a global means of honoring Big-Hearted People. My purpose is to recognize the many acts of generosity and kindness they perform on the behalf of others, which produce great blessings yet often go unnoticed.

Practical recognition can play an important part in our lives. It helps to add value to our accomplishments and confirm that others appreciate our efforts. However, it's the extreme praise of fellow humans and personal hubris that we should avoid. (Hubris: exaggerated pride or self-confidence.[2]) The real takeaway from this is: we should have an attitude of humility and recognize that without God we can do nothing, but we must also recognize that with Him we can do all things. The prophet Isaiah revealed that God especially dwells among those who walk in humility: "For thus says the High and Lofty One Who inhabits eternity, whose name is Holy: 'I dwell in the high and holy place, With him who has a contrite and humble spirit, To revive the spirit of the humble, And to revive the heart of the contrite ones'" (Isa. 57:15, NKJV).

On our next step to discover the path to greatness, we'll observe the life of Jesus, our ultimate role model. From Him we can receive insight to understand that true greatness is not what most people realize.

The Way Up Is Down

Matthew the tax collector (his given name was Levi) saw life through the eyes of a cheat and swindler. In Jesus' day, people despised those of his profession. The apostle Mark describes Matthew's friends as "publicans and sinners." Yet Jesus still chose him by saying, "Follow me," and Matthew left everything to become His disciple.

As a Gospel writer, Matthew gives extended discourses on Jesus' denunciation of the scribes, Pharisees, and Sadducees. In his Gospel, he depicts Jesus upbraiding these phony religious leaders. (See Matthew 5.) No doubt, Matthew could spot a poser from far away—he had plenty of experience as one. These men loved the reverence they received (does the term *reverend* come to mind?)

as moralists, scholars, and teachers. They enjoyed the praise of men more than the praise of God.

In the next chapter, we find Jesus addressing His disciples and the crowds that gathered. He told them to follow their religious leaders' teachings on the Law of Moses but avoid following their example. Jesus described their tendency to do everything for show when He said, "They love to sit at the head table at church dinners, basking in the most prominent positions, preening in the radiance of public flattery, receiving honorary degrees, and getting called 'Doctor' and 'Reverend'" (Matt. 23:7, The Message). Human nature loves to receive honor and hold titles. Even Christians, if not careful, can give in to this temptation. Jesus was well aware of this tendency and spoke these words to His disciples (and to us): "The greatest among you will be your servant. For whoever exalts himself will be humbled, and whoever humbles himself will be exalted" (Matt. 23:11–12, niv).

On another occasion, Jesus' motley (or in contemporary terms, multi-diverse) group of followers were arguing among themselves. Two of them had their mother ask Jesus if they could sit on His left and right hand in His kingdom. Jesus responded by aiming His words at the heart of the matter: "You know

> What some don't understand is that God is the one who gives us all our unique talents and abilities.

that the rulers of the Gentiles lord it over them, and their high officials exercise authority over them. Not so with you. Instead, whoever wants to become great among you must be your servant, and whoever wants to be first must be your slave—just as the Son of Man did not come to be served, but to serve, and to give his life as a ransom for many" (Matt. 20:25–28, niv). There was no mistaking His intent. His words were precise and accurate. He hit the heart-target every time.

Let me point out the word *slave* in this passage, if it hasn't already caught your eye. You might be thinking about why He chose such a strong word. Why didn't Jesus choose to use the word *servant* again? After all, that could have made His point. We find the answer by looking at the historical context.

At that particular time in history, slavery was common and acceptable. The master had complete rule over the slave, even to the degree of life and death. Now, Jesus was not promoting slavery but wanted to stress His point dramatically. In this way, His disciples would realize the depth of service He wanted them to show not only to Him, but for each other as well. He was simply telling them the way up is really the way down. The path to honor and greatness is the servant's path. Yet, words like this fly in the face of common thinking in our world today.

THE POWER TO SERVE?

If you look closely at modern politics, you can easily see the threefold motivation of many who seek political office—power, prestige, and control. Some politicians will do or say whatever it takes for the populace to elect them to positions of power. The "for the people" thinking of our founding fathers has almost completely disappeared. The term *public servant* seems like an obsolete phrase. However, when we also look at corporations and even—sad to say— some churches, the same pattern emerges.

In the business world, serving should be the fundamental philosophy of a corporation. Any business that does not focus on listening to their customers and best serving their needs travels the road to failure. Consumers have stopped buying products from some companies just because of inadequate customer service. The product was superior, but their service to the customer was inferior.

> The path to honor and greatness is the servant's path.

Many consider Albert Schweitzer (1875–1965), theologian, musician, philosopher, and physician, a great man. The world stage honored him with the 1952 Nobel Peace Prize for his reverence for life philosophy. Yet, despite all his accomplishments his perspective on what comprises happiness may surprise you. He said, "The only ones among you who will be really happy are those who will have sought and found how to serve."[3]

Jesus first spoke this truth to His disciples over two millennia ago. It was just before the Passover feast and nearing the time that He was to die. In one of His last teachings, He wanted to stress something extremely important and make it *personal*.

> He got up from the meal, took off his outer clothing, and wrapped a towel around his waist. After that, he poured water into a basin and began to wash his disciples' feet, drying them with the towel that was wrapped around him. When he had finished washing their feet, he put on his clothes and returned to his place. Do you understand what I have done for you?" he asked them. "You call me 'Teacher' and 'Lord,' and rightly so, for that is what I am. Now that I, your

Lord and Teacher, have washed your feet, you also should wash one another's feet. I have set you an example that you should do as I have done for you. I tell you the truth, no servant is greater than his master, nor is a messenger greater than the one who sent him. Now that you know these things, you will be blessed if you do them.

—John 13:4–5, 12–17, NIV

This scene dramatically demonstrates the role of a servant. The only acceptable response is to ponder deeply what Jesus taught us through His selfless act. Jesus as a servant—though He was God in the flesh—washed the dirty feet of sinful men. By this He also foreshadowed His perfect sacrifice, through which He would wash away the sins of humanity by His blood.

This is what the Scripture means when it urges us to have the mind of Christ. In the Book of Philippians, we read that Jesus, "who, being in the form of God, did not consider it robbery to be equal with God, but made Himself of no reputation, taking the form of a bondservant, *and* coming in the likeness of men. And being found in appearance as a man, He humbled Himself and became obedient to *the point of* death, even the death of the cross" (Phil. 2:6–8, NKJV). So by this example we see that having the mind of Christ is:

> The only ones among you who will be really happy are those who will have sought and found how to serve.
> ALBERT SCHWEITZER

- being humble
- being a servant
- being obedient to God

Someone who represents true greatness is my wife, Ruth. She doesn't have a PhD, is not a CEO or head of state, and has never won an Olympic gold medal. However, she is a faithful wife and mother, serving her family, friends, and members of the body of Christ—all because she has a servant's heart. She honors God with her gifts and never places herself above anyone but joyfully takes on the role of a servant. She is a genuine Big-Hearted Person and knows that her greatness comes from God.

Likewise, God calls all of us to be servants—right where we are. Contrary to some people's thinking, you don't need a pulpit to serve the Lord. Whether in the workplace, at school, at home, or at church, we can be a blessing to those we serve. We will be the happiest when we think of others more and ourselves less.

In Matthew 25, Jesus praises His people's faithfulness during their lifetime by saying, "Well done, good and faithful servant…enter into the joy of your Lord" (v. 23, NKJV). Do you notice He doesn't say, "Well done, good and faithful pastor, bishop, prophet, or teacher," but rather uses the word *servant*? He does not recognize our office or gifts, though they are important. He refers to us by what we should be first—servants.

We will be the happiest when we think of others more and ourselves less.

Serving may not seem glamorous or exciting but produces deep joy knowing that God considers it His highest calling. It enables us to see things differently. Serving helps to develop something within our character that is the primary virtue of a servant—humility. Humility is not self-deprecating or allowing oneself to be a doormat or pushover. Humility simply says, "Anything that I am or any gifts or abilities I possess come from God. I'm merely a steward and use them to glorify Him and bless others." The apostle Paul explains this as the source of his confidence when he wrote to the church in Corinth, "Not that we are competent in ourselves to claim anything for ourselves, but our competence comes from God" (2 Cor. 3:5, NIV).

THE CHILD WITHIN

Jesus often used children to explain His message to the disciples and the common people. On one occasion, the disciples came to Jesus and asked, "Who is the greatest in the kingdom of heaven?" (Matt. 18:1, NIV). His answer was 180 degrees out of sync with the current mindset of our day:

> He called a little child and had him stand among them. And he said: "I tell you the truth, unless you change and become like little children, you will never enter the kingdom of heaven. Therefore, whoever humbles himself like this child is the greatest in the kingdom of heaven."
>
> —MATTHEW 18:2–4, NIV

What depth of meaning was Jesus trying to convey? To His disciples and us, Jesus explained that we are to possess these same qualities in our own lives. What qualities do we observe in children? We see sincerity, humility, trust, teachable spirits, and simplicity.

I recall a time when, as a young boy, I walked to our neighbor's house and pulled up some flowers (roots and all) from her garden. I brought them home and proudly presented them to my mom. She smiled and thanked me for being so thoughtful. When she returned them to our neighbor, the woman was not upset at all. On the contrary, she thought it was sweet that I loved my mom enough to give her a special gift. She did not view me as a thief or vandal but as a loving and sincere child. I was innocently sincere in the belief that I was doing something special for my mom. Sincerity carries no pretense, contains no hidden motives, and is transparent.

Children display humility because they don't think they're better than anyone else is and are content just to be themselves. It's not important to them whether they come from royal heritage or from common folks, or if their parents are rich or poor. They don't care if they're more talented or more intelligent than their little friends are. They don't strut their stuff or dress to impress. Little children don't worry about what they will eat, where they will live, or what they will wear. They know that Mommy and Daddy love them enough to meet all their needs. Therefore, their tender hearts know safety, peace, and security. Trust means that it's not necessary for them to have all the answers. They somehow understand that the knowledge, wisdom, or ability of someone greater than them is enough. From this basis, trust forms in their hearts, and they simply rest in that trust.

Children have a wonderful curiosity and are always trying to learn something new. They have a great capacity to listen and will believe what others tell them because they have teachable spirits. Because of this, they can learn so much in a short time. Their minds are like sponges, soaking up every new thing in their learning experience. I don't ever remember seeing a small child who was complex in his or her thinking or actions. There's a certain peace that accompanies them because they are simple—and content to be so. You don't have to go into great detailed explanations to a child. Simplicity is all that's necessary for them to understand and learn.

Sincerity carries no pretense, contains no hidden motives, and is transparent.

As Big-Hearted People, we should desire these childlike heart qualities, because they all play a part in true greatness. However, does this mean we are to be naïve, weak, or allow people to take advantage of us? No! The same Lord who calls us to be like children also speaks to us through the Scriptures reminding us of the following truths:

The righteous are as bold as a lion.

—PROVERBS 28:1, KJV

For God hath not given us the spirit of fear; but of power, and of love, and of a sound mind.

—2 TIMOTHY 1:7, KJV

The weapons we fight with are not the weapons of the world. On the contrary, they have divine power to demolish strongholds.

—2 CORINTHIANS 10:4, NIV

But the people who know their God shall be strong, and carry out great exploits.

—DANIEL 11:32, NKJV

Remember, Jesus, the gentle Lamb of God, is also the mighty Lion of Judah. Through meekness and humility, He became obedient even to death on a cross, but as a result, won the greatest battle ever fought. He took the lowest place as a servant but God the Father highly exalted Him as King of kings and Lord of lords. He conquered this world and Satan and, in so doing, purchased our salvation.

Jesus left His example of greatness for us to follow. Simply stated, if you desire greatness, become a servant.

16

COME TO THE QUIET

He makes me lie down in green pastures,
he leads me beside quiet waters.

—DAVID BEN JESSE[1]

I would like to ask you to start this chapter by performing a simple exercise in audio perception. Close your eyes for a few minutes and listen to the sounds around you.

Perhaps you're hearing music, people talking, or the distant hum of traffic. Some sounds might be loud and harsh, while others, though lower in volume, seem dissonant and annoying. Maybe all you hear are soft, muffled background noises or, if you're fortunate, the pleasant sounds of nature. But something you're probably not experiencing is silence—and that's not surprising. The absence of sound seems strange in our noise-saturated society.

Since the invention of television, radio, and music-playing devices, our need for auditory excitation has dramatically increased. At home, our TVs or stereo systems provide us with enough audio adrenaline to keep us stimulated. While we commute, the radio or CD player pumps out the decibels. And if that's not enough, we're talking on our cell phones. Just watch people outdoors walking, jogging, skating, or riding bikes. Most likely you'll see them listening to media players. Restaurants, stores, and malls not only bustle with activity but also fill our heads with top 40 or golden oldie hits. Driven, intense, repetitious, and even frantic music assaults our ears and souls. The last half century has spawned audio junkies with agitated spirits.

As you will discover in the Appendix, certain vibrations can stimulate our soul and body to promote physical healing and emotional well-being. But if they can affect us positively, then it's obvious they can affect us negatively as well. Certain types of audio stimuli can disturb our spirits and diminish our peace, which is so vital in our walk with God.

Now I'm not suggesting that we should stop watching TV, listening to music, or enjoying other forms of electronic media. If I did, that would produce nothing more than legalistic bondage. We simply need to take a balanced approach. All the modern sound-related inventions I've mentioned, whether acoustic or electronic, also play an important part in my life—especially when it comes to music. However, I still find it necessary to come to the quiet in the Lord's presence to refresh my spirit, soul, and body.

We have grown so familiar to auditory stimulation that some people have even developed a fear of silence. Sound often becomes a method employed to cope with loneliness, suppress unpleasant memories, or deal with the stress-filled aspects of life. However, the silence they're avoiding could possibly be the first step in experiencing freedom from bondage. How do I know? I've been there.

> Certain types of audio stimuli can disturb our spirits and diminish our peace, which is so vital in our walk with God.

Silence plays a significant role in our lives. It enables us to be more attentive, opening our senses to a deeper realization of the beauty of God's creation. Silence encourages rest and helps us to sleep soundly. We can even use it as a way to improve learning. The art of mime uses the mastery of silence to entertain audiences. Poets use the quiet pauses of white space with as much care and meaning as they do words to move our emotions. Silence is an essential component of music, without it, music cannot exist. So it's obvious that silence, though often underestimated, is much more necessary and important than we realize.

While it's difficult to get away from all noise, we can still choose to cultivate an attitude of quietness and stillness before God. But it's not enough just to talk about it or to study it. We need to put it into practice.

In the Book of Revelation, we read a familiar verse often referred to as Jesus giving an invitation for salvation: "Behold, I stand at the door and knock. If anyone hears My voice and opens the door, I will come in to him and dine with him, and he with Me" (Rev. 3:20, NKJV). However, when you read it in context, you find that Jesus was addressing the lukewarm church of Laodicea, who needed to rekindle their passion and dispel their tepid devotion. He asked them to first *listen* to hear His voice, then open their heart's door and participate in a love feast with Him. If you truly yearn for a passionate and satisfying walk with God, then take Jesus' words seriously. Open the door of your heart and remove all that distracts you from fellowship with Him—even "good" things.

The apostle Luke shared an account that begins as Jesus and his disciples make their way along the dusty roads to the village of Bethany. A woman named Martha invited Him to dine at her home. Martha's sister, Mary, sat at Jesus' feet, quietly listening to His every word. But Martha, distracted by all the meal preparations, came to Jesus and asked Him, "Lord, I have all this work to do and my sister hasn't lifted a finger to help. Tell her to get busy!" Jesus answered, "Martha, Martha, you are worried and stressed out about too many things, but there's really only one thing needed. Mary has made the better choice, and it won't be taken from her." (Author's paraphrase from Luke 10.)

Martha had good intentions. It's apparent she had a servant's heart and wanted to make everything perfect for her special guest. But she allowed good things to distract her from the best—spending time with Jesus. And though she didn't realize it, His time on Earth would soon be ending. Had she known, do you think she would have done things differently? I do.

Mary chose to come to the quiet, to sit silently in Jesus' presence and listen to Him. In Psalm 131:2, David figuratively describes a similar, silent posture of his soul before the Lord: "Surely I have calmed and quieted my soul, Like a weaned child with his mother; Like a weaned child *is* my soul within me" (NKJV).

> Open the door of your heart and remove all that distracts you from fellowship with Him—even "good" things.

There is nothing more peaceful than a baby who has just finished feeding and is at rest in his mother's arms. Yet, this is how we begin to experience intimacy with the Lord—by stilling our spirits and resting in His presence.

When my children were young, they often jumped up into my lap as I sat on the couch and would say, "Daddy, tell me a story." So I would gladly share a Bible story or a tale about myself when I was a young boy. On other occasions, they would climb on my lap, lay their head on my chest, and snuggle. I placed my arms around them and gave them a gentle hug and kiss. They wouldn't ask me for anything but just enjoyed my love and affection. Sometimes they would look up at me and say, "I love you, Daddy." It warmed my heart and brought me great joy. (Now I experience the same with my grandchildren.) God wants us to have a similar relationship with Him, to enter His presence and simply enjoy Him.

Yet, enjoying God seems strange to some people because they find it hard to relate to Him as their Father. They derive their view of God as heavenly Father by the example they received from their earthly father. If their fathers were kind, loving, affectionate, and often gave their approval, they derive a normal view of God as their Father. However, if their fathers were austere, critical, and unaffectionate, that's how they view God's fatherly image. The way we can understand our simple child-to-Father relationship with God is to think about what a good, loving father should be like; then realize God is not only like that but also so much more. Discover what the New Testament declares about His fatherly character.

> For the Father Himself [tenderly] loves you because you have loved Me and have believed that I came out from the Father.
> —JOHN 16:27, AMP

> Every desirable and beneficial gift comes out of heaven. The gifts are rivers of light cascading down from the Father of Light. There is nothing deceitful in God, nothing two-faced, nothing fickle.
> —JAMES 1:17, THE MESSAGE

Come before Him in prayer and ask Him to reveal Himself to you as your Father. Allow Him to respond by enabling your spirit to sense His affection, love, and peace.

> It actually brings God great pleasure to fellowship with us. It's humbling to ponder this, but it's true.

It actually brings God great pleasure to fellowship with us. It's humbling to ponder this, but it's true. It doesn't matter if it's for 15 or 115 minutes—just as long as we spend dedicated time with Him alone, that is what's important. But most likely, you'll find the more time you spend with God the more you'll want to spend time with Him. Now, this doesn't guarantee that everything will go perfect throughout the day (as we might view perfection). But it makes us aware of His abiding presence, which we need continually. We are also apt to be more sensitive to His gentle promptings and respond in obedience. And this is necessary if we expect to be effective as Big-Hearted People.

The words of eleventh-century Archbishop Anselm of Canterbury inspire us to shut out the nonessentials and seek God:

> Come now, little man! Flee for a while from your tasks, hide yourself for a little space from the turmoil of your thoughts. Come, cast aside your burdensome cares, and put aside your laborious pursuits. For a little while give your time to God, and rest in him for a little

while. Enter into the chamber of your mind, shut out all things save [except] God and whatever may aid you in seeking God; and having barred the door of your chamber, seek him.[2]

The Bible also encourages us to "seek the Lord and His strength; yearn for and seek His face and to be in His presence continually!" (1 Chron. 16:11, AMP).

The term *seek* does not mean that we are here on Earth, God is in heaven, and we need to get His attention to persuade Him to bring His presence "down to us." As Christians, the presence of Jesus already dwells inside us by the person of the Holy Spirit. (See 1 Corinthians 3:16.) So in the context of Anselm of Canterbury's statement, *seek* simply means to shut out everything else, acknowledge God's presence, and commune with Him. Certainly, this parallels what we find in Hebrews 11:6—God rewards those who diligently seek Him.

I have found the best time of the day for me to fellowship with the Lord is in the early morning. It also sets the stage for the rest of my waking hours. If you are not a morning person, then spend time with him in the evening, maybe just before you go to bed. You'll sleep better and wake up the next morning refreshed and ready to serve the Lord with gladness. Make it a daily habit. Once you do, you'll find that it's the most important part of your day. I usually start out my morning fellowship with God by praise, worship, and thanksgiving. This takes my mind off myself and shifts my focus to the Lord. Then I quiet my soul and wait in silent stillness. I don't ask Him for anything; words aren't necessary.

Now, I readily admit that silence can, indeed, feel uncomfortable. Noise and activity is so common for us that quietness and stillness is at first difficult. Through experience, I discovered I needed to quiet the chatter of my thought life and bring silence to my spirit. Since I have an active imagination, my mind would wander and follow any thoughts that appeared. However, I found the only way to clear my mind was to respond with God's Word.

The Scriptures tell us that through God's weapons of warfare, we can "pull down strongholds and cast down thoughts or imaginations and bring them captive to the obedience of Christ." (See 2 Corinthians 10:4–5.) If you experience drifting and distracting thoughts, then speak these words aloud by faith: "I cast down the imaginations of my mind and bring every thought captive to obey Christ, and I speak peace to my spirit in Jesus' name." You may find that this requires perseverance, but if you're steadfast, you'll experience a calm release and an undisturbed mind and spirit.

Now, most people wouldn't think it strange if you told them you talk to

God. Prayer is a universally accepted form of communication with Him. Yet, if you told them you hear God, they may consider you part of the lunatic fringe. But we see many instances in the Bible in which God spoke to people, sometimes audibly but more often by a gentle impression in his or her spirit. We must remember that God is a Spirit; therefore He communicates directly to our spirit. Our spirit then reveals what God is saying directly to our souls.

Throughout the Bible, we read that God requires us to be obedient to His Word. The Greek word *logos* refers to God's written Word as revealed to us in Scripture. The Bible calls Jesus the Living Word (*logos*) in John 1:1: "In the beginning [before all time] was the Word (Christ), and the Word was with God, and the Word was God Himself" (AMP). *Rhema* is a Greek word that describes God speaking directly to our spirits.

> We must remember that God is a Spirit; therefore He communicates directly to our spirit.

While the logos word is the same for us all, the rhema word for each of us is different. It may give us special insight into scripture, wisdom into specific spiritual matters not addressed in Scripture, and guidance for our daily lives. We receive these special rhema words during our times of intimate communion with the Lord. This is one way God answers the questions we've asked Him, such as:

- Should we buy this house?
- Do I accept this job offer?
- Which college should I attend?
- Should we move to another city?
- Is this the person I should marry?

The rhema word is also how God tells us to show Big-Heartedness by:

- cooking a meal for a shut-in,
- praying for someone in distress,
- giving money to meet a financial need, or
- sending a greeting card to encourage someone.

It's obvious to see our need to have daily, intimate fellowship with the Lord. To become everything God intends for us to be as Big-Hearted People, it is indispensable. The following poem is a simple way to help you remember the highlights of this chapter. May it encourage you to take time and come to the quiet each day.

COME TO THE QUIET

We often ask our Lord to hear
Us during times of prayer,
To fill us with grace and wisdom,
While in His presence there.

But anxious thoughts do overwhelm
Our souls with worldly cares;
We often fail to wait until
His answer is declared.

How can we hear His gentle voice,
With a rushed, frantic pace?
We need to get alone with Him,
In a calm, silent place.

Come to the quiet—be refreshed,
And wait upon His Word.
Lay aside all busyness and
Fellowship with your Lord.

Don't rush—take time to worship Him,
And let your heart proclaim,
His goodness, love, and majesty;
Give thanks and praise His name.

When you spend quiet time with God,
You learn to know Him more;
Then fellowship with Him becomes,
Much sweeter than before.

So with childlike faith, trust Him to
Reveal His perfect will.
You'll find that in His timing, your
Desires He shall fulfill.

—R. J. SCHUM

17

IMPERFECTLY PERFECT

The Holiness of God excuses no sin, but the love
of God forgives all sin through Christ.

—Anonymous[1]

I know I am somebody, cause God don't make no junk.

—Ethel Waters[2]

What this quotation lacks in grammar, it makes up for in deep wisdom. Ethel Waters perfectly described how God views each of us—*as somebody*. He looks beyond our race, gender, or status in society. He loves us all equally because He created us. Unfortunately, fallen humanity does not view its fellow creatures the same. Yet when you search the Scriptures, you see that God delights in raising up people whom the world considers "junk" for His eternal purposes.

> He raiseth up the poor out of the dust, and lifteth up the beggar from the dunghill, to set them among princes, and to make them inherit the throne of glory: for the pillars of the earth are the Lord's, and he hath set the world upon them.
>
> —1 Samuel 2:8, kjv

I purposely used the King James translation because of the word *dunghill*. It stresses that God lifts us out of the heap of stinking waste we make of our lives. He cleans us up, gives us new life, and makes us a blessing to others. Some may take exception to the comparative word *beggar* in this verse by proudly declaring, "I'm no beggar; I've worked hard and have made a good life for myself." Sorry to burst your bubble, but all of us are spiritual beggars in need of God's mercy and righteousness. The Bible is emphatic about this when it says, "There is none righteous, no, not one" (Rom. 3:10, KJV).

I have often used the following words of David in Psalm 40:1–3 as a testimony of what God has done (and continues to do) in my life:

> I waited patiently and expectantly for the Lord; and He inclined to me and heard my cry. He drew me up out of a horrible pit [a pit of tumult and of destruction], out of the miry clay (froth and slime), and set my feet upon a rock, steadying my steps and establishing my goings. And He has put a new song in my mouth, a song of praise to our God. Many shall see and fear (revere and worship) and put their trust and confident reliance in the Lord. (AMP)

God loved me when I was far from Him, living an immoral, rebellious life. After searching for satisfaction in drugs, sex, and other self-destructive habits, I finally gave up. I had no other choice. If I continued walking the same path, I would have perished. I asked the Lord to save me, take control, and change me from within. He reached His hand into the slime of my life, lifted me out of the pit, and set my feet on the Rock, Jesus Christ. The One whom the world refers to as God suddenly became Father to me.

GOD BECOMES A LAMB

God Himself became a sacrifice to atone for the sins of mankind; this is the great truth of Christianity. Through the blood sacrifice of the Lamb of God, Jesus Christ, God works a miracle in a person's life. He makes their dead spirit alive and justifies them (since humanity is born physically alive but spiritually dead). To the pardoned sinner He imparts the righteousness (right-standing) of Jesus Christ. They are no longer condemned sinners but new creations in Christ, fully pleasing to God and free from the judgment and penalty of sin. Christians are the only people who don't have a past, because God wipes their slate clean. It doesn't matter what we were before we came to Christ, He forgives and forgets. This is not someone's opinion, but the truth of God's Word.

> When you search the Scriptures, you see that God delights in raising up people whom the world considers "junk" for His eternal purposes.

> But when the kindness and love of God our Savior appeared, he saved us, not because of righteous things we had done, but because of his mercy. He saved us through the washing of rebirth and

renewal by the Holy Spirit, whom he poured out on us generously through Jesus Christ our Savior, so that, having been justified by his grace, we might become heirs having the hope of eternal life.

—TITUS 3:4–7, NIV

Therefore, if anyone is in Christ, he is a new creation; old things have passed away; behold, all things have become new.

—2 CORINTHIANS 5:17, NKJV

In contrast, other religions require you to do something to merit their god's favor. You need to appease him or her by sacrifice, clean up your life, or perform certain rituals. Then and only then, you might become worthy of acceptance; although there remains a possibility that you could still fall out of favor. Other beliefs center on one's ability to achieve a higher state of consciousness or enlightenment by some prescribed method. This can never fill the spiritual void that exists in all of us. Why? Because it cannot make our spirits alive, which are dead in sin. There is only one way to give life to our spirits and fill our empty hearts—a personal relationship with Jesus Christ. (See the Addendum section at the end of the book.)

I KNOW THAT MY REDEEMER LIVES!

During the mid-1970s, the church that my wife and I attended started an outreach youth ministry. We held it in the basement of the church, so we called it The Cave. Each Saturday night, young people met for praise and worship, teaching, and fellowship. This ministry welcomed anyone, and because of this, it attracted many local youth and a few adults.

One Saturday evening, an unfamiliar African-American man came through the door and later introduced himself as Henry. He was in his early sixties, but surprisingly seemed to fit-in, even among the youth. Years before this, Henry lived an ungodly life as an alcoholic. After stealing a woman's purse, the judicial system convicted him and he served time in New York's Attica Correctional Facility. In September 1971, during his imprisonment, the prison experienced a bloody riot that left thirty-nine people dead. Though he didn't take part in the rebellion, it nevertheless affected him deeply. It was in Attica Prison that Henry, seeing his need for a Savior, turned his life over to Jesus Christ. He became a changed man—from the inside out. After serving his sentence, the correctional facility released him. The post-prison Henry was the one we came to know and love.

We could always expect to hear this humble man share words of encouragement on most Saturday nights. When he stood before us speaking, his countenance seemed to shine with the love of Christ. He always finished his words of wisdom or testimony with the same familiar phrase: "I know—thank God Almighty, I know—that my Redeemer lives!" (Job 19:25). A drunkard and thief became an honest, righteous man through Jesus Christ. Henry's story reflects God's great plan for mankind—redemption, restoration, and glorification. This is the beauty of the Gospel and the wonder of God's love; Jesus didn't call the righteous but sinners to repentance (Luke 5:32).

I'M OK—YOU'RE OK?

Some people think that all their good deeds play a part in their salvation. Maybe they've been active in their church for many years, received the sacraments, and lived morally according to the Golden Rule. Surely God considers good works, right? This quotation by nineteenth-century American educator and theologian Mark Hopkins answers that question directly: "The very act of faith by which we receive Christ is an act of utter renunciation of self and all its works, as a ground for salvation."[3] Our own works, no matter how good, account for *nothing* as it relates to our right-standing with God. Even if we're Big-Hearted People, that in itself doesn't guarantee us a place in heaven.

The following verse gives credibility to the previous statements: "But God had so much loving-kindness. He loved us with such a great love. Even when we were dead because of our sins, He made us alive by what Christ did for us. For by His loving-favor you have been saved from the punishment of sin through faith. It is not by anything you have done. It is a gift of God. It is not given to you because you worked for it. If you could work for it, you would be proud" (Eph. 2:4–5, 8–9, NEW LIFE). Religious works only satisfy man's requirements, not God's. His requirement is perfection, and since none of us is perfect, all hope of salvation by our own works quickly fades.

> Even if we're Big-Hearted People, that in itself doesn't guarantee us a place in heaven.

"Cart before the horse" theology says your good works merit salvation; but thinking like this won't get you anywhere. Although, if you realize your good works result because of your salvation, then you're in for a good ride. I offer the following word picture to help me explain it.

If God placed an advertisement on Earth to attract people who wanted to spend eternity in heaven, what would it say? Maybe this:

Wanted:

Repentant sinners; willing to receive the gift of salvation and eternal life.

Self-righteous need not apply

Once a person becomes born again, good works come because of the indwelling Holy Spirit. You might have heard the saying "Christians aren't perfect, just forgiven." In other words, we are imperfect in ourselves—we still fail, stumble, and sin—but we are perfect in Christ, because through Him we receive His forgiveness. It almost seems too good to be true, but thankfully it's not. We are the imperfectly perfect. How wonderful! A scripture that underscores these thoughts forms the benediction of the single-chapter Book of Jude: "Now to Him who is able to keep you from stumbling, And to present you faultless Before the presence of His glory with exceeding joy, To God our Savior, Who alone is wise, Be glory and majesty, Dominion and power, Both now and forever. Amen" (Jude 1:24–25, NKJV). This verse not only refers to our time here on Earth ("He is able to keep us from stumbling") but eternity as well ("presents us faultless in His presence, with exceeding joy"). How humbling it is to think that we actually bring joy to God's heart.

> How humbling it is to think that we actually bring joy to God's heart.

The Old Testament prophet Zephaniah wrote hundreds of years before Jude and revealed another dimension of God's love: "The LORD your God in your midst, The Mighty One, will save; He will rejoice over you with gladness, He will quiet you with His love, He will rejoice over you with singing" (Zeph. 3:17, NKJV). The Lord rejoices over us with gladness and singing. It's hard for me to picture in my mind God, singing to me with joy, but He does! The following practical example may help us to understand this more fully, especially those who are parents.

My wife and I have three children and seven grandchildren. They always give us joy. Yes, there have been times when they have not obeyed and even disappointed us; yet, we still love them dearly. At times we might not see them for a while, but when we are reunited, there are plenty of hugs and kisses—exceeding joy and rejoicing. If we get so excited about our own family members, how much more excited does God get about us? He loves us far greater than any love we know on this side of eternity.

With these thoughts in mind, we can have confidence that living as Big-Hearted People is not dependent on achieving a certain degree of perfection. Neither do we have to wait until we think we're ready. God will use us as we are and where we are—right now, today! The more we allow the Holy Spirit to conform us to Christ's image, the more Big-Heartedness will become a way of life. Then we can demonstrate it to others, regardless of what we were before or who we are today.

ADDENDUM

The Most Important Decision You Will Ever Make

Maybe some of what you're reading is unfamiliar to you. Perhaps you really don't know how you stand with God. You might attend church faithfully and live an upright, moral life, yet you're unsure where you would spend eternity if you died today. The good news of the gospel is that whomever comes to Jesus, He will not cast out. The Bible states "That if you confess with your mouth, 'Jesus is Lord,' and believe in your heart that God raised him from the dead, you will be saved. For it is with your heart that you believe and are justified, and it is with your mouth that you confess and are saved" (Rom. 10:9–10, NIV). Once you accept the gift of salvation through Jesus Christ, you receive the guaranteed promise of eternal life. It's a done deal, sealed by the Holy Spirit.

> It's in Christ that you, once you heard the truth and believed it (this Message of your salvation), found yourselves home free—signed, sealed, and delivered by the Holy Spirit. This signet from God is the first installment on what's coming, a reminder that we'll get everything God has planned for us, a praising and glorious life.
> —Ephesians 1:13–14, The Message

How can you receive God's gift of salvation? It's simple—so simple many people miss it. Just pray this prayer with sincerity:

> *Dear Jesus, I confess that I'm a sinner. I'm sorry that I have sinned against you and I need your forgiveness. I believe you died on the cross, shed your blood, and rose from the grave to cleanse me from sin. Come into my heart and be my Savior and Lord. Thank you that I am now your beloved child and I will spend eternity with you. Help me to live for you all the days of my life. Amen.*

Now, if you prayed that prayer with sincerity, you have become born again. Congratulations, you're now a new creation in Christ! God forgives all your sins, and He chooses never to remember them. You are free from the penalty of sin.

I would love to hear about your decision to accept Jesus Christ as your Savior and Lord. Please go to the following Web site, select "Contact Us," and send me an e-mail. I have something I want to send you to help you with your walk with God.

Randy J. Schum

www.bigheartedpeople.com

APPENDIX
THE HEALING NATURE OF MUSIC
Diane Schneider, JD, PhD

If we want to experience the miracle of God's creation at work, we need only listen to music. As we do, a complex cooperation occurs between brain and body. Every cell in the body vibrates; from neurons in the brain to the emotion receptor cells that line the intestines. Cells of each organ system have their specific vibratory rate and pitch. When we are ill, depressed, stressed, have undergone surgery, had too little sleep, or experience agitation, our cells in every organ system vibrate differently. They may produce pain, nausea, high blood pressure, and irregular heart rate.

To return cells to their normal, healthy vibratory patterns, I first pray for the patient. I open myself to the care and direction of the Holy Spirit for this person's life and health. Then I choose and sequence certain notes on the harp, certain tempos and rhythms, intervals between notes, chord structures, and plucking techniques directed to that purpose.

While the human voice and many other instruments can also "tone" or drone and then focus in a healing way, the harp is unusual in that it has many strings (usually from twenty-five to forty-seven). The vibrations of each plucked harp string multiply many times by corresponding overtones and undertones. This rich mix and blend of harmonic sound bathes the body, mind, and spirit of a listener with all the vibrational energy the sound carries.

The vibrations from the harp enter through the skin and bones and into the ears and the central nervous system. In this way all the body's cells gently begin to vibrate toward a return to homeostasis and good health. This lowers blood pressure, stabilizes heart rate, relieves anxiety and depression, reduces stress, and encourages deep sleep.

I trust the Holy Spirit to "direct the traffic" between brain and body so whatever is in need of healing within this patient receives healing. I am so grateful, and it always feels like the greatest honor to minister to patients during this most sacred time.

Dr. Diane Schneider has pioneered a protocol using harp vibration therapy with prayer in hospitals and especially with persons at the end of life. For more information about Dr. Diane Schneider's therapeutic harp music ministry, go to www.harpofhope.com.

NOTES

INTRODUCTION

1. William Wordsworth Longfellow, "Tintern Abbey," *3000 Quotations on Christian Themes*, edited by Carroll E. Simcox (New York City: Baker Books, a division of Baker Publishing, 1975).

2. Helen Keller quote accessed at "Word of the Week—Fidelity, 3/31/006," *Georgia Military College*, http://www.gmc.cc.ga.us/wow_archive.html?wow_id=191&wow_date=03/31/2006 on August 24, 2009.

3. Winston Churchill, quoted in *3000 Quotations on Christian Themes*.

4. Charles Dickens, *A Christmas Carol* (Mineola, NY: Dover Publications, 1991).

5. Mother Teresa quote accessed at "Faithfulness and the Fruit of the Spirit," The River Church, www.riverchurch.org.uk/Publisher/File.aspx?ID=17273 on August 24, 2009.

6. Stephen Grellet, quoted in *3000 Religious Quotations*, edited and compiled by Frank S. Mead (New York City: Baker Books, a division of Baker Publishing, 1965).

PART I: SEVEN ATTRIBUTES OF BIG-HEARTED PEOPLE

1. Horace Mann, quoted in *3000 Quotations on Christian Themes*.

CHAPTER 1—KINDNESS

1. Albert Schweitzer quote accessed at "Kindness Quotes," *Stress Relief*, http://www.stresslesscountry.com/kindness-quotes/index.html on September 4, 2009.

2. Victor Hugo, *Les Miserables*, translated by Charles E. Wilbour (New York: Random House, 1992).

3. Ralph Waldo Emerson, quoted in *3000 Quotations on Christian Themes*.

CHAPTER 2—EMPATHY

1. Victor Robinsoll, quoted in *12,000 Religious Quotations*.

CHAPTER 3—COMPASSION

1. Solomon Ibn Gabirol, quoted in *3000 Quotations on Christian Themes*.

2. Albert Schweitzer quote accessed at "Albert Schweitzer Quotes," *ThinkExist. com*, http://thinkexist.com/quotation/the_purpose_of_human_life_is_to_serve_and_to_show/146836.html on September 4, 2009.

3. *Merriam-Webster Online Dictionary*, s.v. "sympathy," accessed at http://www.merriam-webster.com on September 4, 2009.

4. *Merriam-Webster Online Dictionary*, s.v. "pity."

5. "Dictionary and Word Search for *chamal* (Strong's 02550)," *Blue Letter Bible*, accessed at http://cf.blueletterBible.org/lang/lexicon/lexicon.cfm?strongs=02550 on September 4, 2009.

6. "Dictionary and Word Search for *racham* (Strong's 07355)," *Blue Letter Bible*, accessed at http://cf.blueletterBible.org/lang/lexicon/lexicon.cfm?strongs=07355 on September 4, 2009.

7. Modern Language Association (MLA), s.v. "compassion." *Dictionary.com Unabridged* (v. 1.1). Random House, Inc. http://dictionary.reference.com/browse/compassion (accessed September 14, 2009).

8. Dietrich Bonhoeffer, quoted in *3000 Quotations on Christian Themes*.

CHAPTER 4—SELF-SACRIFICE

1. Anonymous quote taken from *3000 Quotations on Christian Themes*.

2. Richard Cecil, quoted in *12,000 Religious Quotations*.

3. St. Augustine, quoted in *12,000 Religious Quotations*.

4. Quote taken from *3000 Quotations on Christian Themes*.

5. Frederick William Robertson, quoted in *12,000 Religious Quotations*.

CHAPTER 5—SELFLESS GIVING

1. Amy Carmichael quote accessed at *QuotationsBook.com*, http://quotations-book.com/quote/24439/ on September 4, 2009.

2. Anonymous poem excerpted from *12,000 Religious Quotations*.

CHAPTER 6—UNCONDITIONAL LOVE

1. William Blake, taken from *A Poem A Day*, edited by Karen McCosker and Nicholas Albery (Hanover, NH: Steerforth Press, 1999), 242.

2. Victor Hugo, quoted in *12,000 Religious Quotations*.

CHAPTER 7—SENSITIVITY TO PEOPLE'S NEEDS

1. *Merriam-Webster Online Dictionary*, s.v. "sensitivity."

2. "Dictionary and Word Search for *brabeuō* (Strong's 1018)," *Blue Letter Bible*, http://www.blueletterbible.org/lang/lexicon/lexicon.cfm?Strongs=G1018&t=KJV (accessed September 4, 2009).

CHAPTER 8—THE HEALING POWER OF FORGIVENESS

1. Jean Paul Richter, quoted in *3000 Quotations on Christian Themes*.

2. Don Colbert, M.D., *What You Don't Know May Be Killing You* (Lake Mary, FL: Siloam, 2004), 84–85.

3. Mark Twain, quoted in *12,000 Religious Quotations*.

CHAPTER 9—THE FREEDOM OF SIMPLICITY

1. Thomas à Kempis, GIGA Quotes, http://www.giga-usa.com/quotes/authors/thomas_kempis_a002.htm (accessed September 25, 2009).

2. St. Francis of Assisi, "The Peace Prayer," http://www.wf-f.org/StFrancisAssisi.html (accessed September 25, 2009).

3. "Dictionary and Word Search for *haplotēs* (Strong's 572)," *Blue Letter Bible*, accessed at http://www.blueletterBible.org/lang/lexicon/lexicon.cfm?Strongs=G572&t=KJV on September 4, 2009.

4. "Dictionary and Word Search for *aperispastōs* (Strong's 563)," *Blue Letter Bible*, accessed at http://www.blueletterBible.org/lang/lexicon/lexicon.cfm?Strongs=G563&t=NIV on September 4, 2009.

5. Mohandas Gandhi quote accessed at *Experience Life* magazine online, http://www.experiencelifemag.com/issues/april-2009/whole-life/live-simply-so-that-others-may-simply-live.html on September 3, 2009.

6. Jean Baptiste Henri Lacordaire, *Lacordaire*, accessed at Google Books, http://books.google.com/books?id=TKATAAAAYAAJ&pg=PA89&lpg=PA89&dq=Henri+Lacordaire+What+our+age+wants+most+is+the+sight+of+a+man,+who+might+possess+everything,+being+yet+willingly+contented+with+little.+For+my+own+part,+humanly+speaking,+I+wish+for+nothing.+A+great+soul+in+a+small+house+is+the+idea+which+has+touched+me+more+than+any+other.&source=bl&ots=MbrWXqUfXs&sig=3dCzlakhBjXqQ_abO5J1RQspB2I&hl=en&ei=3NOfSpipDKD8tgfJupj1Dw&sa=X&oi=book_result&ct=result&resnum=1#v=onepage&q=&f=false on September 3, 2009.

CHAPTER 10—THE RICHES OF CONTENTMENT

1. Thomas Aquinas, quoted in *12,000 Religious Quotations*.

2. Phillips Brooks, quoted in *Elbert Hubbard's Scrap Book* (Gretna, LA: Pelican Publishing Co., 1923), 48, accessed at Google Books, http://books.google.com/books?id=N7cl1lUSMugC&pg=PA7&lpg=PA7&dq=elbert+hubbard's+scrap+book&source=bl&ots=e3NccV6ilk&sig=CazyGccZJCkgkCqyWBW7LaB9Ib8&hl=en&ei=IlShSrf_F5qJ8QbjrZXfDw&sa=X&oi=book_result&ct=result&resnum=10#v=onepage&q=&f=false on September 3, 2009.

3. William Shakespeare's *Henry VI*, Part III, may be found at http://shakespeare.mit.edu/3henryvi/3henryvi.3.1.html (accessed September 3, 2009).

CHAPTER 11—IT'S THE LITTLE THINGS

1. Julia Fletcher Carney, "Little Things," *Bartleby.com*, accessed at http://bartleby.com/100/527.html on September 3, 2009.

CHAPTER 12—SIMPLY ORDINARY

1. Angélique Arnauld, quoted in *12,000 Religious Quotations*.

CHAPTER 14—PRAYING FOR DEAR LIFE

1. Charles Delucena Meigs, quoted in *12,000 Religious Quotations.*
2. Phillips Brooks, quoted in *12,000 Religious Quotations.*
3. *Merriam-Webster Online Dictionary,* s.v. "supplication."
4. "Dictionary and Word Search for *amēn* (Strong's 281)," *Blue Letter Bible,* accessed at http://www.blueletterBible.org/lang/lexicon/lexicon.cfm?Strongs=G281&t=KJV on September 4, 2009.

CHAPTER 15—THE GREATEST

1. Ralph Waldo Emerson, quoted in *3000 Quotations on Christian Themes.*
2. *Merriam-Webster Online Dictionary,* s.v. "hubris."
3. Albert Schweitzer, quoted at "Advancing Chaplaincy: NACC Volunteers," *National Association of Catholic Chaplains,* http://www.nacc.org/volunteers/ (accessed on September 4, 2009).

CHAPTER 16—COME TO THE QUIET

1. Psalm 23:2, NIV.
2. Archbishop Anselm of Canterbury, quoted in *3000 Quotations on Christian Themes.*

CHAPTER 17—IMPERFECTLY PERFECT

1. Anonymous quote excerpted from *12,000 Religious Quotations.*
2. Ethel Waters, quoted in http://pacafour.blogspot.com/2007/11/wonderfully-made.html (accessed September 14, 2009).
3. Mark Hopkins, quoted in *12,000 Religious Quotations.*

TO CONTACT THE AUTHOR

www.bigheartedpeople.com

Free companion study guide download available